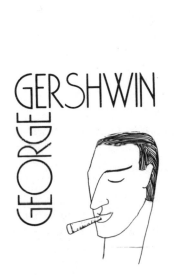

True music . . . must repeat the thoughts and aspirations of the people and the time. My people are Americans. My time is today . . .

George Gershwin

Whether we like it or not, it is in that great bargain sale of five and ten cent lusts and dreams that the new bottom level of our culture is being created.

John Dos Passos

GERSHWIN

GEORGE

A BIOGRAPHY BY
ALAN KENDALL

HARRAP

London

ACKNOWLEDGEMENTS

The author and publishers are grateful to the following for permission to reproduce material in this book:

Illustrations:
Atheneum Press: pictures of William Daly, Mabel Schirmer and Rosamond Walling Tirana, reproduced from *The Gershwins* by Robert Kimball and Alfred Simon (1973). Glyndebourne Festival Opera: picture of 1986 production of *Porgy & Bess*. Photograph by Guy Gravett. The Raymond Mander & Joe Mitchenson Theatre Collection: pictures used on endpapers; picture of Fred Astaire and Adele Astaire from *Lady, Be Good* (bottom picture); two pictures from production of *Primrose*. Popperfoto: picture of George and Ira Gershwin boarding an aeroplane to California. Gabriel Hackett, G.D. Hackett Agency, USA: all other illustrations (including those on the front and back cover).

Text:
Frank Magro for permission to quote from Osbert Sitwell's *Laughter in the Next Room*, pp.179-80. The lyrics of 'Where's That Boy?' p.120 – © 1928 New World Music Corp. – are reproduced by kind permission of Chapell Music Ltd., London.

Every effort has been made to trace copyright owners of prose extracts used in the text and any omissions will be rectified in future reprints.

First published in Great Britain 1987
by HARRAP Ltd
19-23 Ludgate Hill, London EC4M 7PD

Copyright © Alan Kendall 1987

ISBN 0 245 54332-5

Designed by Kirby-Sessions, London
Phototypeset by Falcon Graphic Art Ltd
Wallington, Surrey
Printed and bound in Great Britain
by Mackays of Chatham

Contents

Introduction

'Gershwin is a leader of young America in music, in the same sense in which Lindbergh is a leader of young America in aviation.' This quotation comes from a speech made to accompany a presentation to the composer after the first performance of *An American in Paris*. For most of those present on that occasion, it would probably have been true to say that Gershwin was *the* leader of young America in music. He was then thirty, with several successes behind him, and several more still to come before his life was tragically cut short in 1937.

That speech was made in December 1928, and as the Twenties drew to a close, it seemed as if Gershwin had, through his music, brilliantly caught the mood and the very spirit of the decade. Perhaps it was inevitable that in the next decade Gershwin should have gone to Hollywood, and that he should have died there. But this is much too much of a simplification, because it was also in the Thirties that Gershwin wrote what many regard as his greatest achievement, the opera *Porgy and Bess*.

To Otto Kahn, who made the speech, Gershwin was standing at some sort of a crossroads at the end of 1928. Again, for most of the people present on that occasion, there was probably no earthly reason why Gershwin should not have gone on in exactly the same way, pouring out his tunes as before. However, Kahn — and one or two others — felt that Gershwin was capable of better things, but that he needed to undergo some emotional experience in order to inspire or release them. Kahn, it must be mentioned, was chairman of the board of the Metropolitan Opera, and his particular interest was that Gershwin might write an opera, but there were also others, such as conductors and critics, who felt that he might be the

7

composer who would lead serious, 'classical' American music to its rightful place in the concert hall.

That, in terms of music history, was the crux of the Gershwin phenomenon. Was he a composer of popular music who somehow wandered into the realm of serious music, for which he was simply not equipped, and was then drawn up into the great American dream of success and fame — or was he a gifted songwriter who became carried away by his own ambition when he ought to have accepted his limitations? Accepting his limitations would not, of course, have prevented Gershwin from having ideas and inspiration; it was more a question of how and where they were directed. In the opinion of many critics he never wrote anything more than tunes, even in his extended 'serious' works, and the ability to write a good tune was his supreme talent. He was also a highly accomplished pianist — though in performance of his own music — and his pianistic technique was a major influence and stimulation in the articulation of his musical thoughts.

One cannot divorce the music from the man, however, and when one hears of, and reads, diametrically opposed reports of his behaviour towards others, one senses that the two strands in his personality were complemented by the two strands in his music. Some people only ever saw him as charming, sensitive and generous, whereas others saw him as rude, overbearing and arrogant. He was capable of being both kinds of personality, even to those who were regarded as old friends. Again, was he an innocent who was swept up in the great American quest for success, or did he seek that success from the outset, and pursue it in spite of all the odds? Certainly once he tasted success, it became a major concern, and in his public pronouncements at least, he indicated that he had no doubts about his talents and success. One also knows, however, that at times he felt very deeply about adverse criticism, and that he was assailed by doubts, to the verge of paranoia.

From this point of view it was particularly significant that he never formed a deep relationship, let alone married, and that apart from one or two members of his family, his closest relationships tended to be with working colleagues, or grew out of what were initially working relationships. Towards the end of his life, especially, one feels that a wife would have given him the support he needed, and possibly even induced him to take the necessary steps that would have diagnosed his fatal illness much sooner. That might not have averted the tragedy, but his existence might have been prolonged, and he would have had comfort at a particularly distressing time.

There is a deep paradox, therefore, in the life of George Gershwin, that the man who came to epitomise America in music, with all its brashness and its sentiment, its glamour and its emotion, remained a curiously lonely and emotionally unfulfilled figure who excites our sympathy, even pity, rather than admiration or envy. But for the pleasure that his music has given to millions of people across the world, in the end it is our gratitude that is extended for the life and works of George Gershwin.

1 ARRIVAL

Arrival

By the end of the nineteenth century, New York was the most cosmopolitan city in the world. It has been estimated that there were already more Italians living there than there were in Florence and Venice put together; three times more Irish than in either Dublin or Belfast; the equivalent of two-thirds of the population of Berlin for Germans — or almost the populations of Hamburg and Munich taken together — and more Russians than the population of Kiev.

A symbol of the welcoming hand extended to the rest of the world was the Statue of Liberty, at the entrance to New York harbour, unveiled in 1886, and the gift of the Republic of France to the American people in commemoration of the centenary of the Declaration of Independence. In fact, the full symbolic significance of the statue is Liberty Enlightening the World, which is a slightly different proposition from that of Liberty pure and simple, but for many immigrants it has been, almost more than anything else, the enduring symbol of the country of their hoped-for adoption. Those arriving by ship would rush to the rail to gaze on it, and so it was that, only some five years after its inauguration, a young Russian emigré did likewise, and in so doing lost his hat in the waters of New York harbour. Presumably the hat itself was a matter for regret, but more worrying must have been the fact that tucked in the band of the hat had been the address of an uncle, his only contact in America, and so with it went the emigré's sole point of contact in the New World.

With perseverance, of course, the young Russian soon tracked down Uncle Greenstein the tailor, despite the fact that he had no English, for in that cosmopolitan city Yiddish and Russian did almost as well in certain quarters, so that eventually he reached Brooklyn and his uncle, and so embarked on his career in his new country. Nor was he to remain alone for long, since the young girl

13

he had already fallen in love with in Russia had preceded him with her parents, and sooner or later he would track her down, too, in New York, and marry her within some three or four years of his arrival. Though he never made a fortune for himself, he was to achieve considerable fame as the father of several gifted children, one of whom was to become, in his short life, one of America's greatest composers.

Morris (Moishe) Gershovitz emigrated from St Petersburg (Leningrad), in the early 1890s, possibly to escape conscription, and adopted the spelling Gershvin, then eventually Gershwin, soon after his arrival in America. He married Rose Brushkin (Bruskin) on 21 July 1895, though they had known each other previously in St Petersburg, as we have already seen. Ira, their first child, was born on 6 December 1896, and George, their second, on 26 September 1898. In fact, the first name on Gershwin's birth certificate was Jacob, after his paternal grandfather — the idea of George came later. In a similar way Ira always assumed that his first name was Isidore, since he was called 'Izzy' by family and friends, until he applied for a passport in 1928 and discovered that the name on his birth certificate was Israel.

Ira said that George and he had once tried to remember exactly how many different houses, flats and apartments they could recall in their early days, and reached a total of more than twenty-five. They seemed to move every time their father took up a new occupation, which on George's birth certificate is given as 'leather worker', but at one time or another he was the owner or operator of restaurants, Russian and Turkish baths, bakeries, a cigar store and pool parlour, a bookmaker's, and rented accommodation. Most of Ira and George's early boyhood was spent on the lower East Side of Manhattan. There were two other children: Arthur, born on 14 March 1900, and Frances, born on 6 December 1906.

Of the parents, Rose seems to have been by far the more important and influential figure as far as the boys were concerned, and indeed this is consistent with the traditional role of the Jewish mother. In 1931 George described her as 'nervous, ambitious and purposeful', and although she was never a doting mother, according to him, she was nevertheless loving, and determined that her children should have a proper education. Her belief was that if all else failed, they could always become teachers. But George did not do well at school, and despite the prospect of her son becoming a musician and earning $15 a week playing a piano for the rest of his life, she consented when he asked to leave high school at the age of fifteen and take a job as a pianist and song-plugger at Remick's.

Already it had become apparent that George had musical talent, and despite his street-kid bravado — to which a scar over his right eye was a lasting testimony — music had taken hold of him. He himself recalled that one of his first positive musical memories dated from the time he was six, as he stood outside a penny arcade in Harlem, on 125th Street, 'in overalls and barefooted', and listened to an automatic piano playing Rubinstein's *Melody in F*.

One may well question the accuracy of George's detail about being barefoot, since Rose always maintained that they were never without a maid at any time in their somewhat precarious existence of those early days, and when she attended the première showing of *Rhapsody in Blue*, the film of Gershwin's life, in 1945, she was heard to remark that they were never as poor as depicted. On the other hand, Ira recalled taking Rose's diamond ring to the pawn-shop and redeeming it on no less than five or six occasions, thus raising about $400 each time.

Then we have recollections of the occasion at Gershwin's school at the time, P.S.25, during which an eight-year-old violinist, Maxie Rosenzweig — later known as Max Rosen — played Dvořák's *Humoresque*. In fact, Gershwin was not in the hall for the performance, but heard it through a window. Nevertheless, he was so moved that he immediately determined to get to know Rosenzweig, two years his junior. He waited for him after school in the pouring rain for an hour and a half, without success, so found out his address and, wet as he was, presented himself at the door. Maxie had been and gone, but his parents were so impressed by Gershwin's determination that they arranged for the two to meet. It must have been a severe blow to Gershwin to learn that, in the younger boy's opinion, he had better give up any idea of a musical career, since he simply did not have the necessary musical ability. In element Rosenzweig was right, and in some ways the rest of Gershwin's relatively brief career may be regarded as a struggle, despite popular acclaim, to compensate for that lack of fundamental ability.

Even when, in 1910, the Gershwins bought a second-hand upright piano on hire purchase, it was not for George that they did so, but for Ira, as the oldest son. Yet from the start it was George who commandeered the piano, and soon left Ira in the shade. As the latter recalled:

The upright had scarcely been put in place when George twirled the stool down to size, sat, lifted the keyboard cover, and played an accomplished version of a then popular song. I remember being particularly impressed by his swinging left hand and by harmonic and rhythmic effects I thought as proficient as those of most of the pianists I'd heard in vaudeville.

George's explanation as to how he came to be so proficient seemed, Ira noted, all very simple. Whenever the opportunity presented itself he had been using a schoolfriend's player piano (pianola). Whatever the truth of the matter, though, there is no reason to doubt the veracity of what Gershwin said — his proficiency persuaded his parents to let him take proper piano lessons.

His first teacher was a Miss Green, in the neighbourhood, at fifty cents a lesson, and from her he progressed to a Mr Goldfarb, of Hungarian origin, who charged three times as much, and encouraged his pupils to play selections from opera, rather than make them tread the path of scales and exercises. Even at that stage Gershwin realized that Mr Goldfarb's gestures and gusto were no substitute for real technique, and when in 1912 a pianist friend, Jack Miller, suggested that Gershwin should meet his own teacher, Charles Hambitzer (1891–1918), Gershwin readily agreed. By way of showing what he could do at the first encounter, Gershwin played the overture to *William Tell* after the manner of Mr Goldfarb. When he had finished, Hambitzer is supposed to have commented: 'Let's hunt out that guy and shoot him — and not with an apple on his head either.'

Hambitzer was enormously important in Gershwin's career, and seems to have recognized his pupil's potential at an early stage. In a letter to his sister Olivia, written shortly after the start of giving lessons to Gershwin (for which he took no fee), Hambitzer foretold his pupil's future:

The boy is a genius, without doubt; he's just crazy about music and can't wait until it's time to take his lessons. No watching the clock for this boy. He wants to go in for this modern stuff, jazz and what not. But I'm not going to let him for a while. I'll see that he gets a firm foundation in the standard music first.

16

For his part, Gershwin maintained that Hambitzer was the first great musical influence in his life and the person who made him 'harmony-conscious' — though apparently no more than that. In encouraging Gershwin to attend concerts regularly, Hambitzer helped Gershwin to form the habit of 'intensive listening'. The most positive result of this was that Gershwin became, in his own words, 'saturated with the music', and when he got home he sat down at the keyboard and played over passages from memory.

It was Hambitzer who suggested that Gershwin should go to Edward Kilenyi (1884–1968) for additional lessons in theory, saying: 'The boy is not only talented, but is uncommonly serious in his search for knowledge of music.' It is all the more regrettable, given the interest that Hambitzer took in Gershwin's education, that he died in 1918, though presumably Gershwin had stopped having lessons from him some time before that.

In 1912 Gershwin had entered the High School of Commerce, to study accountancy, but even there he played the piano at morning assembly, and in the summer of 1914 or possibly 1915 he found a job as a pianist at a resort in the Catskill Mountains at the princely salary of $15 a week. By 1913 Gershwin had already written two songs, to words by Leonard Praskins — 'Since I found You' and 'Ragging the Träumerei' — and on 21 March 1914 he made his first public appearance as pianist and composer at the Finley Club, a literary group in affiliation with the City College of New York, of whose entertainment committee Ira was a member. George's piano solo listed on the programme on this occasion was another of his unpublished pieces, a tango. His performance in accountancy at the High School of Commerce was by no means so accomplished, however, and two months later, in May 1914, he left school and took his first steps of his career as a professional musician. Through a friend, Ben Bloom, he had been introduced to Mose Gumble, manager at the Jerome H. Remick Music Company, in the area known as Tin Pan Alley. Soon George had been offered a job; Rose Gershwin gave her consent, and at the age of fifteen, George left school to become one of the youngest pianists in the trade, at a salary of $15 a week.

The lyricist Irving Caesar recalled of that time:

Remick's was an amazing place. There was always something happening. Performers would be there to hear new songs for their acts, and it was a real beehive of rehearsal activity.

17

George was a much sought-after accompanist there. They all loved to have George play the new songs for them. He was like a salesman exposing the inventory, and the songs were inventory. He was a great salesman because the way he played the piano was unique.

This facility at the keyboard was to stand Gershwin in good stead as a springboard, not only for his entrée into the musical profession, but also as the way in which he would eventually articulate his musical thoughts, drawing them out of himself. It also became a matter for pride, and he grew to expect that people would want to hear him play, and became positively offended if they did not. He never really learned how to read from sight, however, even relatively late in his career, though with such a talent, one must confess, that hardly mattered.

There was a great deal of money to be made from popular music — as indeed there has been increasingly throughout the twentieth century — but in the days before radio, television and mass record and cassette sales, the money came chiefly from the sale of sheet music. To ensure success for a song, therefore, it had to become widely known so that people would want to go out and buy the music. In order to do this, publishers employed song salesmen or 'pluggers', whose job it was to induce singers, instrumentalists and variety acts to perform the songs wherever and whenever possible, but mostly in theatres, bars and restaurants. Inevitably pluggers would often resort to bribery in one form or another, cheer and clap if they were present at a performance, or even hire a *claque* to do so.

It would have been cruel and unrealistic to have subjected such a young and inexperienced person as George Gershwin was in 1914 to this kind of activity, so initially he spent most of his time in one of the several cubicles at Remick's, playing the songs published by the company for eight or more hours a day to anyone who came to listen. As he said of that time:

Every day at nine o'clock I was there at the piano, playing popular tunes for anybody who came along. Colored people used to come in and get me to play 'God Send You Back to Me' in seven keys. Chorus ladies used to breathe down my neck. Some of the customers treated one like dirt.

But he did not spend all his time in his cubicle. Mose Gumble, the manager, sent him out on occasion to vaudeville houses to check that tunes published by Remick's were being used in certain acts, and at other times he would go around cafés and restaurants with a group of singers and dancers — and not only in New York — 'plugging' Remick songs.

Gershwin's time at Remick's was an invaluable experience in view of where his future lay. He saw at first hand how the popular music world worked and its less attractive aspect. He would never be a starry-eyed, innocent young composer trying to get some kindly publisher to buy his work. Then, from a purely practical point of view, the long hours spent at the keyboard gave him great flexibility in transposition, and greatly enhanced his technique both as an accompanist and performer. He soon became one of the best pianists at Remick's, and members of the profession specifically went to hear him play. Fred Astaire — né Austerlitz — recalled of 1915:

> I would go to the various music publishers looking for material, and George was a piano player demonstrating songs at Jerome H. Remick's. We struck up a friendship at once. He was amused by my piano playing and often made me play for him. I had a sort of knocked-out slap left hand technique and the beat pleased him. He'd often stop me and say, 'Wait a minute, Freddie, do that one again.'
>
> I told George how my sister and I longed to get into musical comedy. He in turn wanted to write one. He said, 'Wouldn't it be great if I could write a musical show and you could be in it?'

That dream finally came true when Fred and Adele Astaire were in *Lady, Be Good*, which opened at the Liberty Theater in New York on 1 December 1924.

As the conversation with Fred Astaire reveals, even at this stage Gershwin was beginning to think of himself as a songwriter, and the following year, on 15 May 1916, the publisher Harry von Tilzer, on the recommendation of Sophie Tucker, agreed to take what became Gershwin's first published song: 'When You Want 'Em, You Can't Get 'Em — When You've Got 'Em, You Don't Want 'Em', to lyrics by Murray Roth. Roth was happy to accept $15 for his part, but Gershwin stuck out for royalties, and wanted an advance against them. Von Tilzer gave Gershwin $5 from his pocket, and that was all he ever earned from the song. Even so, it is interesting that such a professional as Sophie Tucker, to whom Gershwin had played the song, had been sufficiently impressed by it to bother to recommend it to Harry von Tilzer. She knew that the latter would not have taken kindly to having his time wasted, and she was to some extent putting her own reputation behind the song.

By this time Gershwin had discovered a means of supplementing his income at Remick's, which was by making pianola rolls. On Saturdays George would go out to East Orange, New Jersey, and make rolls at $5 each or $25 for six. He had a great admiration for the comedian Ed Wynn, which may have finally induced him to adopt the ending 'win' to his name instead of 'vin', but which certainly gave him inspiration for the pseudonym Bert Wynn for some of the pianola rolls he made. There were other names too, such as Fred Murtha and James Baker, which Gershwin may have used either to conceal his own identity for when he became famous, or so as not to give the impression that one person was monopolizing the market. By May 1916, however, Gershwin was plainly listed in a catalogue of rolls issued by the Universal Music Company, and his photograph appeared along with those of six other pianists who played for the company. Between 1915 and 1926 he made at least 125 of these rolls, and by far the greater part of them for the Aeolian Company.

After selling their song to Von Tilzer in 1916, Gershwin and Roth wrote a second one, 'My Runaway Girl', and that was the end of their association. The song was not published, but Gershwin felt that it had show potential, and so took it along to the office of Shubert productions, where it was heard by Sigmund Romberg, who was then the Shuberts' chief composer. Rombert suggested that Gershwin might work with him on his next production, *The Passing Show of 1916*, which was to open on 22 June that year, at the Winter Garden. Gershwin took along several numbers, of which Romberg selected 'Making of a Girl', with lyrics by Harold Atteridge. Schirmer's bought the song, and the following January Gershwin received $7 in royalties, though officially credit for the song was ascribed to both Gershwin and Romberg.

Nevertheless, Gershwin's career was moving in the right direction, and in September 1916 he made a piano roll of what was to be his first published instrumental composition, written in collaboration with Will Donaldson, 'Rialto Ripples'. His own employers, Remick's, published it in 1917, but on 17 March that same year

Gershwin left the company. He put it in this way: 'It was now that the popular-song racket began to get definitely on my nerves. Its tunes began to offend me. Or perhaps my ears were becoming attuned to better harmonies.' Perhaps his sensibilities were not quite so refined at the time he left Remick's, and one suspects that Gershwin was looking at things very much from the standpoint of his later eminence, but undoubtedly he was undergoing a development. As he put it: 'Something was taking me away . . . as I look back, it's very clear that I wanted to be closer to production-music of the kind Jerome Kern was writing.' He had heard two numbers from Kern's *The Girl from Utah* played at his Aunt Kate's wedding, and so became aware that: 'Kern was the first composer who made me conscious that most popular music was of inferior quality and that musical-comedy music was made of better material.'

It was one thing to give up his job at Remick's, but another to find something with which to replace it. One of the songwriters in the firm, Herman Paley, who was also a pupil of Hambitzer and Kilenyi, had befriended Gershwin, and introduced him to his family. Paley advised George to try and interest T.B. Harms, the music publishers, since they had a reputation for encouraging young talent, and Paley's brother Lou wrote lyrics for several Gershwin songs. Later this was to prove a fruitful line to pursue, but before it did, Gershwin had to try other less congenial approaches. It is possible that the summer engagement referred to earlier as having taken place in 1914 or 1915 is in fact to be dated to this period; then he also acted as accompanist for the banjo player Fred Van Eps, who played at parties. In 1917 Gershwin joined a small instrumental group for three or four weeks in a Brooklyn night-club.

But in the last analysis it was all vital experience, and gave Gershwin an insight into the many facets of the immense world of popular music from the ground upwards.

Another source of support and encouragement at this stage was the black composer and arranger, Will Vodery, with whom Gershwin had by this time struck up a friendship. Vodery was to orchestrate the original version of the 1922 one-act opera *Blue Monday Blues*, later entitled *135th Street*, and arrange music for some of the Gershwin shows. At this point, however, he tried to give Gershwin some very practical help, and helped him obtain a post as pianist at Fox's City Theater, at a salary of $25 a week. The appointment lasted for exactly one night, for which Gershwin was

21

never paid. Since he was reading at sight, he missed his cue, and found himself playing one thing as the girls on stage were singing something else. The show's comedian was quick to make capital out of the disaster, and began to make fun of Gershwin's piano-playing, drawing ridicule from the audience in so doing. As soon as the show ended, Gershwin left the theatre and the job, without even claiming any money.

Before long, however, he found more congenial employment, and in July he began working at the Century Theater for $35 a week as a *répétiteur* for the show *Miss 1917*, with a musical score by Victor Herbert and Jerome Kern. Now he was getting near to his idol. The opening night on 5 November was recorded by Ira in his diary: 'A glorious show — entertaining every minute.' Even so, the show ran for only forty-eight performances, but Gershwin had made such an impression during the rehearsals that he was kept on the payroll after the opening night, and acted as accompanist for a series of Sunday evening concerts at the Century Theater, starting on 11 November, given by members of the cast. On 18 November, George played for Arthur Cunningham, and on 25 November for Vivienne Segal, who generously took Gershwin onto the stage for a bow. Even more to the point was the fact that she had sung two of Gershwin's songs, and a representative from Remick's who was present recommended one of them, 'You-oo Just You', for publication, which occurred in 1918. Irving Caesar, who wrote the words, was to become another regular Gershwin collaborator. The other song, 'There's More to the Kiss than the X-X-X', was used by Gershwin for the shows *Good Morning, Judge* and *La, La, Lucille*, both of 1919, thus establishing a pattern that persisted throughout his life that he never wasted his material.

During the closing weeks of 1917, Gershwin worked as an orchestra pianist for an all-Spanish revue using the music of Quinito Valverde at the Cocoanut Grove Roof of the Century Theater. It opened on 6 December and ran for thirty-three performances, of which Gershwin played approximately half.

The Vivienne Segal concert played an important part in assisting the next step in Gershwin's career, since it was also attended by Harry Askins, the manager for *Miss 1917*. Askins had already formed a very favourable impression of Gershwin during the run up to the opening night, and when he heard the two songs that evening, was inspired to mention him to Max Dreyfus, head of T.B. Harms, which had also been singled out earlier, as we saw, by the

Paleys as a likely house for Gershwin. Dreyfus and Gershwin met, and in February 1918 the young composer, as he now was to be regarded, joined the staff. He was to receive a salary of $35 a week, but if a song was accepted by the company, he was to receive an advance of $50, and then a royalty of three cents per copy sold. As Ira somewhat laconically observed in his diary on 10 February that year: 'This entails no other effort on his part than the composing, they not requiring any of his leisure for plugging nor for piano playing. Some snap.'

Before committing himself to Harms, George had already been working as an accompanist with Louise Dresser, for a tour of the Keith theatre chain, which he wished to fulfil, since Louise Dresser was already a singer of national reputation. They opened at the Riverside on 25 February, and went on to play in Boston, Baltimore and Washington. One of the songs which Louise Dresser sang on the tour was one written by her brother Paul, 'My Gal Sal', which Gershwin disliked intensely, as the singer recalled:

> I knew it, but oh! how he played it. There were times when I almost forgot the lyrics listening to Georgie trying to make that trite melody sound like a beautiful bit of music. It wouldn't have surprised me one bit had he banged the piano one day and walked off the stage. I wouldn't have blamed him too much, but that lovable, shy lad wouldn't have done such a thing.

It had nevertheless been a most useful experience for Gershwin to work with such a talented performer.

Gershwin continued to take on such relatively humble tasks as *répétiteur* work for musicals, which in 1918 included Jerome Kern's *Rock-a-Bye Baby* and the *Ziegfeld Follies of 1918*, with music by Louis Hirsch. He also took up the saxophone, though less in order to extend his musical accomplishment than to be able to join a military band rather than the infantry, were he to be conscripted. As it turned out, the Armistice of 11 November 1918 took away that threat. In June his song 'You-oo Just You' was included in the show *Hitchy-Koo of 1918*, which ran for only sixty-eight performances, and September saw the publication of his first song with Harms: 'Some Wonderful Sort of Someone', to lyrics by Schuyler Greene. The song soon caught the attention of Nora Bayes, who wanted to include it in her new show *Look Who's Here*, but the

23

eventual title of the show, with book and lyrics by Harry B. Smith and music mainly by A. Baldwin Sloane, became *Ladies First*. By the time it had its pre-Broadway try-out at the Trent Theater, in Trenton, New Jersey, it had a second Gershwin song included in it: 'The Real American Folk Song', with lyrics by Arthur Francis, alias Ira Gershwin. Thus it was that the Gershwin team of lyricist and songwriter first arrived on Broadway, at the Broadhurst Theater on 24 October 1918, though 'The Real American Folk Song' was dropped during the New York run. The show ran for 164 performances, after which it went on a six-week tour for which Gershwin acted as Nora Bayes' accompanist.

Because she was a star in her own right, Nora Bayes apparently suggested to Gershwin that he should change the ending of a song to please her. He refused, despite the fact that she had induced Irving Berlin and Jerome Kern to do such a thing for her and she had had no problem with them. One is reminded of the stormy interview between Beethoven and Baron von Braun over the failure of the revised version of *Fidelio*. When the baron pointed out that even Mozart had not thought it beneath himself to write for the galleries, which were filling up now, Beethoven retorted that he did not write for the galleries, demanded his score back, and left. It was not only Miss Bayes' demands, however, which upset Gershwin, but the discovery of the sums A. Baldwin Sloane was receiving in royalties; for in later life he was usually quite happy to accommodate his singers in this way. The young Gershwin was not going to accept that his music should merely be interpolated into someone else's show. He was going to ensure that he had his own.

When Gershwin went back to the Harms office, Max Dreyfus had news of an opportunity for Gershwin to write, if not exactly a full score, than at least something more than interpolations. The result was a show entitled *Half Past Eight*, which opened on 9 December 1918 at the Empire Theater in Syracuse, but which never made it to New York. Ira collaborated — as Arthur Francis — on one of the songs, and lyrics for the other three were by Edward B. Perkins, who mounted the show. Despite the disaster, the young Gershwin had some very useful experience of the problems of writing and producing musicals in those early days.

The review of the show, dated 11 December (1918), which appeared in *Variety*, makes quite entertaining reading, in its sardonic tone. It gives praise where praise is due, but points out several good reasons why the show was not a commercial success.

24

By far the largest portion of blame, however, is laid on the shoulders of one person, Edward B. Perkins:

> Perkins, who isn't thirty, is owner, manager and director of *Half Past Eight*. He 'directed' the dress rehearsal from the orchestra pit, the balcony, the stage, and the gallery. Every time the cast thought they had him located he popped up at another place in the theatre.
> Perkins was in Paris one week before the armistice was signed. In the interval that had elapsed, Perkins hit the trail to America, bringing *Half Past Eight*, which has run nine months in London.
> George Gershwin, who wrote the music for it, was also in Syracuse for the dress rehearsal and the opening.
> Perkins graduated from Columbia University six years ago, and is the youngest international theatre magnate in the world. If he keeps up his present speed, he'll be old inside of three months.

As it happened, Perkins went down with 'flu, having worked himself to the point of exhaustion, and several of the members of the cast, worried about their salaries, refused to perform at a matinée. The show closed, and the performances that had been planned for Rochester and Chicago were abandoned.

As a curiosity of this period, Gershwin wrote a patriotic song entitled 'O Land of Mine, America', to lyrics by one Michael E. Rourke, which concealed one of Jerome Kern's lyricists, Herbert Reynolds. He submitted it anonymously for a competition sponsored by the New York *American*, and the prize was $5,000. The jury — including, among others, Irving Berlin, John McCormack, John Philip Sousa and Josef Stransky — did not award the prize to Gershwin, but he received an honorable mention and a consolation prize of $50, as announced in the issue of the *American* dated 2 March 1919.

The excursion into patriotism may well only have been the lure of the $5,000 prize, but Gershwin now had a goal in life — to have his own musical — though before it happened he still had to see more of his songs interpolated into other people's shows during 1919.

The first was *Good Morning, Judge*, with a book by Fred Thompson based on Pinero's *The Magistrate*. Produced by the Shuberts at the

Shubert Theater on 6 February 1919, the music was mainly by Lionel Monckton and Howard Talbot. There were two Gershwin songs, however. The second show, which opened on 12 May, was *The Lady in Red*, with book and lyrics mainly by Anne Caldwell.

Still Gershwin had to wait another two weeks to have the satisfaction of his own Broadway show, but by now it was well on the way. Apparently Jerome Kern, whom Gershwin had known for at least two years at this point, and whom he had so idolised as a composer of musicals and what Gershwin regarded as good songs, had promised Gershwin that when it came to his first musical, he would be more than willing to help him. The reason why Gershwin did not accept his offer is not entirely clear, but it seems that Kern had done something which the producer Alex A. Aarons took as a snub, so that when Aarons came to produce Gershwin's first solo musical he discouraged Gershwin from enlisting Kern's help. Naturally this upset Kern, who thought that the young composer was rejecting him. The two remained cool toward each other until 1922, when Kern declared that he would retire and give Gershwin his show contracts that remained unfilled. In fact he did neither of these things. One can understand why Kern should have felt put out over the Aarons affair, and one has a certain amount of sympathy with Gershwin, who had to remain on good terms with his producer. How far Kern was touched, however, was revealed by the remark ascribed to him: 'Here's Gershwin, who showed a lot of promise.' Ira regretted — since he was present on that occasion — that he did not retort: 'Here's Kern, who promised a lot of shows.'

If things went wrong with Kern at this point, then there was some compensation for Gershwin in the friendship that began with Irving Berlin, who had recently severed his association with his publishers, Waterson, Berlin and Snyder. In 1919 he was to establish his own firm, but before he did so, he toyed with the idea of joining up with Max Dreyfus at T.B. Harms. One day he offered a song to Dreyfus entitled 'That Revolutionary Rag', but he needed someone to take it down. Dreyfus produced Gershwin, who took down the song and played it back to the composer with his own touches. Gershwin knew that the established composer was looking for a musical secretary, and so stated quite openly that he wanted the job. Berlin asked Gershwin what he really wanted to do, and the latter admitted that he wanted to write songs. After listening to some of his songs, Berlin retorted: 'What the hell do you want to work for anybody else for? Work for yourself.' Gershwin was doing just that.

26

2 WELCOME TO BROADWAY

Welcome to Broadway

With the Great War over, the West seemed poised to embark on a period of celebration and relaxation, and although the Twenties were not quite the carefree time that they have often been depicted, there was inevitably a sense of relief and a feeling that a milestone had been passed as the second decade of the century drew to its close. And as the century began to spread its wings, so did the composer who was only a year or so senior, for on 26 September 1919 Gershwin was to celebrate his twenty-first birthday. He was still only twenty, therefore, when on 26 May 1919, he finally made it to Broadway with *La, La, Lucille*, a bedroom farce, the first show for which he wrote all the songs. In fact it was the first musical to be mounted at Henry Miller's Theater. The book was by Fred Jackson, with lyrics by Arthur Jackson and B G 'Buddy' De Sylva (1895–1950), and Gershwin had been chosen by the producer, Alex A. Aarons, in preference to a more established composer. Aarons himself had started out selling clothes, made some money at it, and so decided to try his hand at producing. Admittedly a famous songwriter would have cost considerably more than Gershwin at this stage in his career, but at the same time it says much for the way in which he had impressed Aarons, and this was the start of a working relationship that lasted until 1933. In choosing Gershwin, Aarons had also gone against the advice of his father, Alfred E. Aarons, a very experienced manager and producer, whose confessed method of writing popular and successful songs — or so it was stated in an article in the *New York Telegraph* — was to borrow melodies from Mascagni, Verdi and Wagner. At all events, *La, La, Lucille* ran for 104 performances, and was only stopped because of the actors' strike which closed all the New York theatres in August 1919.

La, La, Lucille, which was described as 'The new up-to-the-minute musical comedy of class and distinction', tells the story of John Smith, a dentist, who becomes heir to a fortune of two million dollars, on condition that he divorce his charming wife Lucille. The money had been left by an eccentric aunt from Boston, who had never approved of Lucille because she had been connected with the stage prior to her marriage. So as to be able to inherit the money and live happily ever after, John and Lucille devise a plan whereby they will divorce on grounds of adultery, and then remarry. The chosen adulteress is Fanny, a janitor's wife, and she and the Smiths find themselves for two of the show's three acts in the hotel where the deed is to take place. Inevitably there are various hitches and complications before the Bostonian aunt appears to reveal that she is not dead at all, but simply playing a joke on her nephew and testing his love for his wife.

Not, perhaps, the most inspiring stuff for a musical by today's standards, but Brooks Atkinson pronounced that the music was: 'now vivacious and surprising of detail, and again harmoniously pleasing'. In fact, two of the numbers had already been used — namely, 'There's More to the Kiss than the X-X-X' in *Good Morning, Judge*, earlier in 1919, and 'The Ten Commandments of Love' came from *Half Past Eight*. 'Nobody But You' was of even earlier vintage, and came not from a show, but from Gershwin's days at Remick's, and the use of all three illustrates one of his enduring practices throughout his career — namely, that he never threw away a good song.

Individual Gershwin songs were also included in other Broadway shows of 1919, and one of them — 'Swanee' — was to become his first smash hit, though one would not have known this from its reception when it was first heard. The occasion was the opening of the Capitol Theater cinema on 24 October 1919, and it was an interesting comment on the times that it was felt either necessary or desirable to present a revue on stage in addition to the feature film that evening. But then the whole genesis of the song was clear demonstration of the truth that success may well come in unexpected ways.

Gershwin and his lyricist Irving Caesar wanted to try and cash in on the one-step 'Hindustan', which was then all the rage. However, instead of an exotic foreign setting they decided to turn to a very American one, the Deep South of Stephen Foster's 'Swanee

River'. Even the title of the song was borrowed in part. Nevertheless, they worked together one evening at the Gershwin apartment in Washington Heights, with Morris Gershwin joining in on a comb wrapped with tissue paper. At this point the poker players in the dining-room, who had initially complained at the noise of composition which was interrupting their game, had no option but to approve the evening's work. The producer of the *Capitol Revue*, Ned Wayburn, made 'Swanee' into a production number, and also included another Gershwin number, 'Come to the Moon', to lyrics by himself and Lou Paley. But 'Swanee' itself might well have sunk without trace, had not Gershwin been lucky enough to meet Al Jolson at a party after the revue ended its run, and been able to play the song for the great entertainer. Jolson took to it and introduced the song into his own show, *Sinbad*, music mainly by Sigmund Romberg, which was running at the Winter Garden Theater. It was an instant success, and on 8 January 1920 he recorded it for Columbia Records. Within a year it is estimated that both Gershwin and Caesar earned in the region of $10,000 in royalties from 'Swanee', and in an attempt to capitalize on its success, they wrote a similar song in conjunction with 'Buddy' De Sylva. However, although Jolson used it in *Sinbad* too, and changed its name from 'Dixie Rose' to 'Swanee Rose', it had nothing like the same impact. There was a particular way in which Jolson had taken hold of 'Swanee' that made it a unique combination of singer and song that no one else was able to emulate, let alone improve on. And for Gershwin himself, it was a turning point in his career. When he went to England in 1923, this was brought home to him vividly, as he wrote to Ira:

> A funny thing happened yesterday which made me very joyful and for the moment very happy when I came here. The boat was in dock at Southampton and everyone was in line with their passports and landing cards. When I handed my passport to one of the men at a table he read it, looked up and said, 'George Gershwin, writer of "Swanee"?' It took me off my feet for a second. It was so unexpected, you know. Of course I agreed I was the composer . . . I couldn't ask for a more pleasant entrance into a country.

There was one more show before the end of 1919 into which Gershwin tunes were interpolated — namely, *Morris Gest Midnight*

31

Whirl, produced by Morris Gest, which opened at the Century Grove on top of the Capitol Theater on 27 December, and which ran for 130 performances. The book and lyrics were by Buddy De Sylva and John Henry Mears, and Gershwin contributed six songs, only two of which were published — 'Poppyland' and 'Limehouse Nights'. Nothing was quite as successful that year, or for some time to come, as 'Swanee'.

But if 1919 was the year of Gershwin's first popular hit, it was also the year of one of his earliest surviving attempts at 'serious' composition — namely, a movement for string quartet which Gershwin entitled 'Lulluby' (*sic*) on the piano sketch in the Library of Congress. *Lullaby*, as it is usually known, is a short movement in which a theme is repeated in somewhat episodic manner with little or no development. Moreover, there is little evidence of awareness on the composer's part of the requirements of stringed instruments — it could equally well have been intended for almost any combination of instruments. And yet to condemn it as 'naive' in both form and content is to judge Gershwin by critical standards totally inappropriate to his experience and development at this stage in his career. The wonder is surely that he wrote it at all, when the whole thrust of his career had been towards writing 'good' popular music.

What is more to the point is that in order to facilitate that writing, Gershwin had been studying round about this time with Kilenyi, and had been doing some basic harmony exercises with him. In fact there is a very short one, dated August 1919, entitled 'String Quartette' — now in the Library of Congress, along with the others. There is nothing much there to analyse in the hope of detecting signs of future genius. At the most the collection of sketches shows how Gershwin tended to take a theme and develop it in certain ways, and how he tended to use material and not waste it. This applies particularly to *Lullaby*, for subsequently he drew on it and incorporated it into the one-act jazz opera *Blue Monday Blues* of 1922, as we shall see.

It is the existence of such a work, however, that gives ammunition to those who maintain that Gershwin was a 'serious' composer who never made it, and superficially the facts can be used to support such a claim, for he himself had a curious obsession with the idea of studying music in the traditional, academic way. Unfortunately, he seems to have lacked the application required to persevere with such a discipline, and this factor, coupled with his

32

Morris and Rose Gershwin, photographed about the time of their marriage in 1895.

Rose Gershwin, at right, with nursemaid and her three sons – photograph taken in a Brooklyn park around 1900. The boys are, from left to right, Arthur, George and Ira.

George Gershwin in his teens, about the time he left school — in May 1914, when he was still only fifteen — and became 'probably the youngest piano pounder ever employed in Tin Pan Alley'. Exactly a year later his first song was published by the Harry von Tilzer Music Publishing Company, a rival to his own firm of Jerome H. Remick & Company, who employed him strictly as a pianist, and not as a writer.

Charles Hambitzer, George Gershwin's first piano teacher.

The offices of Jerome H. Remick & Company on Tin Pan Alley where George Gershwin had his first job. Tin Pan Alley is in fact a nickname for that part of West Twenty-eighth Street, just off Fifth Avenue, between Broadway and Sixth Avenue. In finding work here, Gershwin had come to the very heart of the New York music publishing business, and was excellently placed to launch himself in a career in popular song writing — provided he could make the right people listen.

The dapper George Gershwin in his
early years in Tin Pan Alley, possibly
around the time of *Half Past Eight* in
late 1918. The show was not a success,
but provided Gershwin with some
useful experience early in his career.

Gershwin working for Max Dreyfus at T.B. Harms, the company he joined as a
composer in February 1918, having left Remick's in March the previous year.
During the months between jobs Gershwin worked as an accompanist in a variety
of shows and clubs, thus extending his experience of the very varied aspects of the
world of popular music in and around New York.

A scene from *La, La, Lucille,* 1919, the first musical for which Gershwin wrote all the songs. Members of the cast, from left to right, are J. Clarence Harvey, Alfred Hall, Eleanor Daniels, and the two leading characters played by John E. Hazzard and Janet Velie. As one of the critics wrote: 'There was pretty music by someone named George Gershwin and several pretty girls to dance to it.'

It was thanks to Al Jolson (centre) that Gershwin — in bowler at right — had his first great popular success and financial reward with the song 'Swanee'. Jolson heard it at a party and introduced it into his show *Sinbad,* for which most of the music had been written by Sigmund Romberg, and after the revue for which Gershwin had originally written the song had ended.

Below: William Daly, possibly Gershwin's oldest and most trusted friend, as photographed by the composer. The three *Preludes for Piano*, published in 1927, were dedicated to Daly by Gershwin in recognition of all that he owed him.

Below: The Paul Whiteman orchestra in its augmented form for the concert at the Aeolian Hall on 12 February 1924, when Gershwin's *Rhapsody in Blue* was heard for the first time with the composer at the piano.

Above: Gershwin with Alex Aarons on the boat from London to New York after *Primrose* in 1924. During the trip plans were advanced for *Lady, Be Good*, which was the first complete musical by George and Ira Gershwin to open on Broadway, and the first production by the team of Aarons and Freedley, in December 1924.

Song. "Wait a Bit, Susie." Hilary and Joan.

HILARY: "Susie finds that waiting pays."
JOAN: "I suppose I could learn something from Susie."

Above and below: Gershwin's *Primrose* opened at the Winter Garden Theatre, London, on 11 September 1924, with a cast that included Heather Thatcher, Leslie Henson, Margery Hicklin, Percy Heming, Vera Lennox and Ernest Graham.

The opening of the score of *Rhapsody in Blue*, signed by George Gershwin and dated 7 January 1924, the date on which he began the main draft of the work. What he produced here was in essence a two-piano version, with the two top staves representing the jazz band, and the bottom two staves the piano, which has not entered yet, and so the part is blank. It was from this version — completed round about 25 January — that Ferde Grofé (inset) made his orchestration of the rhapsody. It was completed on 4 February 1924, in the space of ten days, and rapidly became a hit, and the music for which Gershwin is possibly most remembered today.

Above: Fred Astaire, surrounded by chorus girls in the show *Lady, Be Good*, in which he and his sister Adele (below) starred. It opened at the Liberty Theater in New York on 1 December 1924, and ran for 184 performances. Otto Kahn was induced to put $10,000 up as backing for the show on the strength of hearing 'The Man I Love', though it was dropped after only a week of the out-of-town trial-run in Philadelphia. Also in the show was 'Fascinating Rhythm'.

In late July 1925, Gershwin went to stay at Chautauqua, New York State, where Ernest Hutcheson held master classes for piano. At this time Gershwin was working on what was to become his *Concerto in F*, and enjoyed being able to isolate himself or have the company of the students. Standing behind the seated Hutcheson are Jerome Rappaport, Gershwin, Oscar Wagner and Abram Chasins, whilst seated on the ground are Mary Huggins (left) and Muriel Kerr (right).

Mabel Schirmer (*née* Pleshette), studied with Charles Hambitzer, so knew Gershwin from very early days, and remained a lifelong friend and confidante. His letters to her — particularly during the closing months of his life — provide a moving testimony to Gershwin's unhappiness in Hollywood.

Kay Swift, with her husband James F. Warburg, whom she married in 1918. A talented composer in her own right, Kay Swift met Gershwin in 1925, and though her marriage lasted another nine years, it was clear that she recognized in Gershwin not only talent, but a personal sympathy which never left her. Despite all the help she gave Gershwin, especially at the time of *Porgy and Bess*, by the time she was free to marry again, he no longer seemed to regard her as a potential partner in matrimony. However, he dedicated his *Song-Book* to her.

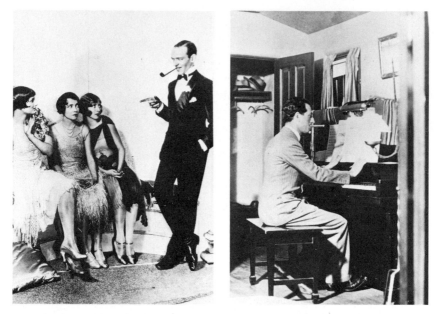

Above left: Fred Astaire with, from left to right, Betty Compton, Adele Astaire and Gertrude McDonald in *Funny Face*, which opened on 22 November 1927, and ran for 244 performances. It celebrated the opening of the Alvin Theater, the home of the Aarons and Freedley shows from this time on.

Above right: During 1925, when there were too many people and too much noise at the house on 103rd Street, Gershwin retired to a couple of rooms at the Whitehall Hotel on 100th Street and Broadway. Here he worked on *Tip-Toes*, *Song of the Flame* and *Concerto in F*.

Gertrude Lawrence in *Oh, Kay!*, which opened at His Majesty's Theatre in London in 1927 after a run of 256 performances in New York. Gershwin was in London for the final performance on 24 March 1928. It was Gertrude Lawrence's rendering of 'Someone to Watch over Me' that linked her name for ever with the musical — her first American-produced show.

Opposite: Gershwin looking over the *Concerto in F* with Walter Damrosch, who commissioned the work, prior to its first performance at Carnegie Hall on 3 December 1925.

Gershwin at the keyboard in Paris in 1928, with his hands in close-up (inset). His visit to Europe in 1928 — but especially the time he spent in Paris — set the seal on his international reputation, and was an eloquent testimony, from the reception given to him by distinguished musicians almost everywhere he went, to what he represented for them. He personified young American music, and inspired several composers. Ironically the music he composed as a result of the trips he made to Paris — *An American in Paris* — owed precious little to any inspiration he himself drew from Europe.

After the unsuccessful opening of *Strike Up the Band*, which opened at the Broadway Theater in Long Branch, New Jersey on 29 August 1927 and closed out of town, Gershwin took a vacation in Florida, where his success as an angler was greater than that as a composer. However, in its revised form, *Strike Up the Band* had much more success in 1930.

Gershwin in Vienna in April 1928, when he met Franz Lehár and Emmerich Kálmán. When he entered the Café Sacher with the latter, the band struck up *Rhapsody in Blue*. By way of contrast, he attended a performance of Ernst Krenek's *Jonny spielt auf* at the Vienna Opera, and took away an inscribed copy of Berg's *Lyric Suite* from his meeting with the composer.

Above: Seated on the *banquette* in the Café Sacher in Vienna in May 1928 are Ira and Leonore Gershwin, George Gershwin, and Emmerich Kálmán. It is said that the chef attempted to produce blue ice-cream to match *Rhapsody in Blue* played by the band, but when that was a failure, he made do with miniature American flags planted in the ice cream.

Below: Gershwin at the races in Havana with Emil Mosbacher in February 1932. The Cuban music — especially the percussion — that Gershwin heard on this visit inspired the *Rumba*, later known as *Cuban Overture*, which he wrote during the July of that year.

arrogance and ambition as success came within his grasp, probably ensured that he never would master it. After all, he had come this far on his own, and he had assembled his own assets, taking what appealed to him where he found it, and as he was able to assimilate it. And it seems that throughout his career it was the element of improvisation — at the keyboard — that produced the results, and not an intellectual, creative act. At the time that he wrote *Rhapsody in Blue* (1924), Gershwin knew (according to Isaac Goldberg) 'as much harmony as could be found in a ten-cent manual', and the composer himself admitted that many of his chords 'were set down without any particular attention to their theoretical structure. When my critics tell me that now and then I betray a structural weakness, they are not telling me anything I don't know.'

What is certain is that Gershwin approached a succession of distinguished musicians from Ravel to Schoenberg, via Varèse and Bloch, and they, for the most part, turned him down as politely as they could. Even so, we have evidence of definite study with professional 'serious' musicians after he left Charles Hambitzer. There was, for example, Artur Bodanzky (1877–1939), a conductor at the Metropolitan Opera, and, as we have already seen, Edward Kilenyi, the Hungarian-born composer, arranger and conductor, with whom Gershwin worked from time to time between 1919 and 1921, and the exercises that he did are now in the Library of Congress. There were all of three lessons with Rubin Goldmark in 1923, and others with Wallingford Riegger, Henry Cowell and Joseph Schillinger, for about four years from 1932. Schillinger was the most lasting by far of Gershwin's teachers, but even there it is easy to see that at least part of the explanation lay in the fact that as Gershwin's career advanced and he was taken more seriously, he felt the need to pay lip service to elements of theory, composition and orchestration as understood in the traditional, classical music world. Back in the heady years of 1919 and 1920, looking at the way in which his career was taking off at that moment, however, and given Gershwin's ambition and desire for success, it is more realistic to assume that he quickly sensed where the way ahead was set to lead him — there would be time for 'serious' music later, if need be.

For those around him, it must have been a happy time. He had a devoted circle of friends still, despite the fact that he was soon to catapult into society. The lyricist Lou Paley was one of the fixed points in Gershwin's world at this time, along with his brother

Herman Paley, who was basically a Tin Pan Alley writer, but had studied with Edward MacDowell (1861–1908) and Hambitzer. There was the Paleys' cousin, George Pallay, and Lou Paley's fiancée Emily Strunsky. When Lou and Emily married in 1920 their Greenwich Village apartment became a favourite rendezvous on Saturday evenings for the Gershwin circle. It was there that Ira met Emily's sister Leonore, whom he eventually married on 14 September 1926. But it was George who was the focus of attention, especially when he sat down to play and sing at the piano. Howard Dietz and his wife, who lived below the Paleys, and initially came to complain that their chandelier was shaking because of the noise, stayed to be entertained and so became regulars. Groucho Marx was another frequent visitor.

But inevitably Gershwin was being taken up into a different world, and one of the most important influences in this respect was that of Jules Glaenzer, an executive at Cartier, whom the composer first met in 1921. Glaenzer took exception to the cigar that seemed to be continually in Gershwin's mouth, and which he neglected to remove even when talking to women. He managed to convince Gershwin that it was not polite to gobble down his food as though he had not had a proper meal in days, and he impressed upon him the wisdom of sticking to one kind of alcohol, rather than accepting and draining whatever was offered to him. Glaenzer also took a hand in Gershwin's choice of clothing, and in short seems to have played Professor Higgins in relation to Gershwin's Eliza Doolittle — or Aphrodite to Pygmalion's statue, perhaps. It was at a Glaenzer party that Gershwin played the song 'Do It Again', which Irene Bordoni heard, was captivated by, and eventually introduced into the show *The French Doll*, in 1922.

Glaenzer took pride in having the cream of international society at his parties, both in Paris and in New York, and liked to introduce them to any new talent whenever possible. He readily gave himself the credit for having groomed several celebrities for fame and stardom, and without hesitation asserted that Gershwin was his 'best pupil' — though in fact it had been Dorothy Clark, then a pianist for Ziegfeld, who took the composer to a Glaenzer party in 1921, along with Vincent Youmans. Glaenzer quickly took up Gershwin, and in 1923 invited him to stay with him in Paris, at 5 rue Malakoff. Buddy De Silva was also a guest on this occasion, which included, as one of its highlights, a visit to a brothel. No doubt Gershwin's boasting induced Glaenzer and De Sylva to indulge in an act of voyeurism that did credit to neither of them.

They subsequently maintained that Gershwin had such a reputation — which he had helped to build — as a ladykiller, that they
expected to see a magnificent 'performance' from the composer.
Instead they saw a highly perfunctory accomplishment of the act,
with the professed sexual athlete displaying none of his expected
skills, and even less enjoyment. Of course, they maintained, he
gave a very different account to his companions afterwards,
completely unaware of what had happened. No one comes out of
the episode with any credit, least of all Glaenzer and De Sylva, who
were of course unable to disclose to Gershwin what they had done.
Furthermore, it would be unwise to draw too many conclusions
from the incident, though it undoubtedly fits into the overall
picture of Gershwin's relations with the opposite sex, which seem to
have been much less highly coloured than the public were led to
believe — by both the press and Gershwin himself, it would
seem — as time went by.

Increasingly Gershwin was to come into a much more sophisticated society than the one in which he had grown up, and as his
fame began to grow, he became a frequent guest at parties where he
met many of the most attractive women of his day. In time some
women almost threw themselves at him, and yet he never seemed to
take advantage of their offers, nor to find the right sort of partner
with whom he felt able to settle down. This is often a problem of
Jewish men whose mothers have filled the traditional matriarchal
role. They find it extremely difficult to form a relationship with a
woman, no matter how much they may wish to do so. In
Gershwin's own case there was the Jewish *chutzpah*, too, which gave
him the urge to make good, and in such a programme there is not a
great deal of time to devote to romance, especially if that involves
courting a woman and offering her attentions and building a
relationship. All too often, as women tended to find to their cost,
Gershwin felt that it was more or less an honour for them that he
took an interest in them, and he offered them an entirely one-sided
relationship in which a girl-friend was simply an adjunct to himself.
By the time he came to realize that he needed a much more
committed relationship, it was virtually too late.

Whatever Gershwin's real attitude to and need for women, it was
through the medium of the glamour revue that he made the next
leap forward in his career. Florenz Ziegfeld (1867–1932) had
inaugurated his *Ziegfeld Follies* in 1907. Under the caption 'An

American Institution', they ran for twenty-four consecutive editions, trading very much on his slogan 'Glorifying the American Girl'. In fact, his recipe was largely that of the *Folies-Bergère* in Paris, but he made the Ziegfeld girl the symbol of perfect American beauty for over thirty years, and in this domain greatly influenced the choice of female stars in the early motion pictures.

It was this market that the Broadway dancer turned producer George White was hoping to cash in on when he produced his *George White's Scandals of 1919*, which opened on 2 June that year. It did not stand up to the competition from the *Ziegfeld Follies*, but White had nevertheless established that opposition was at least possible, and at the start of 1920 Gershwin went to see White in Detroit to try and secure the commission for the score of the next production of *Scandals*. In fact, this was not as long a shot as might at first appear, since Gershwin had already met White when he was a rehearsal pianist for *Miss 1917* and White was a dancer in the show. The latter had felt that one of the contributory factors in the comparative failure of the *1919 Scandals* had been Richard Whiting's score; and Gershwin's increasing reputation, coupled with first-hand experience of him at work in the theatre, convinced White that Gershwin was his man. In the end he wrote the music for five *Scandals* between 1920 and 1924, though the series ran — with some interruption — until 1939.

Possibly in the wake of popular success and first attempts at writing 'serious' music, Gershwin enrolled in some summer courses at the music department of Columbia University in 1921. The courses were given by Rossetter G. Cole, head of the department and a teacher and composer much under the influence of Franck. During the winter months he held theory classes at the Cosmopolitan School of Music in Chicago. Gershwin attended two of Cole's classes that summer, 'Nineteenth-Century Romanticism in Music', and 'Elementary Orchestration', which was designed to cover the historical development of the orchestra, the study of the technical possibilities and tonal qualities of each instrument of the modern orchestra, the principles of tone combination and the arranging of given compositions for various groups of instruments and for full orchestra. Since this class began at 8.30 a.m. one wonders how many of the sessions Gershwin managed to attend. Had he been able to take full advantage of what was offered, however, it would have stood him in good stead as he progressed to more ambitious composition, because orchestration is one domain where controversy still rages around Gershwin. It is interesting that amongst the sketches in the Library of Congress, there is one dated 15 September 1921 which shows interest in writing for the clarinet, and others with the string writing already referred to, but there is nothing to indicate that Gershwin made any headway with orchestration at this period, or for that matter for some time to come, and even then to a questionable degree. But given the amount of effort that he was devoting to his career in the theatre at this time, it cannot have been easy for him to find much room for study when it was not a top priority for him.

Gershwin received a weekly salary of only $50, then $75, for the *Scandals* of 1920, but by 1924 he was earning $125, though this was augmented by royalties when songs from the shows were published. There were not many of these, though 'I'll Build a Stairway to Paradise' (1922) brought Gershwin over $3,000, and 'Somebody Loves Me' (1924) even more. It is said that when Gershwin asked White for a rise, they parted company. In retrospect the association with the *Scandals* was more important for the way in which it gave Gershwin more practical experience in the theatre, and the concomitant development of his reputation, than for financial considerations. And it also had one important aspect as far as his artistic development was concerned, as we shall see. However, Gershwin had not put all his eggs in one basket with the George White *Scandals*, for in 1920, 1921, and again in 1922, he contributed songs to various Broadway shows. The first of these was *Dere Mable*, about Bill, the letter-writing soldier, who was fond of his dog: when it was felt that a song was required for him to sing to his canine companion, the result was Gershwin's 'We're Pals', to lyrics by Irving Caesar, who also provided another lyric for a Gershwin song for the show, 'Yan-Kee'. The hit 'Swanee' was also used in *Dere Mable*, but even with such a draw, the show was never a success. It opened at the Academy of Music in Baltimore on 2 February 1920 and closed out of town.

Next came *Ed Wynn's Carnival*, which opened at the New Amsterdam Theater on 5 April and ran for sixty-four performances. There was only one Gershwin song in this show, 'Oo, How I Love to Be Loved by You', to lyrics by Lou Paley. By contrast, there were no less than seven Gershwin numbers in *George White's Scandals of 1920*, which opened at the Globe Theater on 7 June and ran for 318 performances. Perhaps because of the growing Gershwin success, Anne Caldwell agreed to the interpolation of a

37

Gershwin song into her *The Sweetheart Shop*, which opened on 31 August at the Knickerbocker Theater that year, despite the fact that she had a contract specifically banning such interpolations into her own score. Of course, she had used two Gershwin tunes in her *The Lady in Red* the year before, and her new show ran for fifty-five performances as opposed to the forty-eight of the previous one — but it was still nothing to compare with the *Scandals* runs. But the song itself — 'Waiting for the Sun to Come Out' — is chiefly of interest because it was the first published song written by both George and Ira, though the latter still used Arthur Francis as his pseudonym for the authorship of the lyrics.

There was one more show of 1920, *Broadway Brevities of 1920*, which included three Gershwin songs, and starred Eddie Cantor. Opening on 29 September at the Winter Garden, it ran for 105 performances.

In 1921, Ira, still as Arthur Francis, wrote the lyrics for seven Gershwin tunes for a show entitled *A Dangerous Maid*, though only five were used in the final version. Despite Vivienne Segal and Vinton Freedley in the cast, the show never reached Broadway. It opened on 21 March in Atlantic City and closed in Pittsburgh in May, but true to his fashion Gershwin salvaged one of the unused numbers, 'The Sirens', and used it later in London in *Primrose* (1924) as 'Four Little Sirens'. The 1921 *George White's Scandals* were not as successful as those of the previous year, only managing a run of ninety-seven performances, though five out of the six Gershwin numbers in the show were published. By way of contrast, an Ed Wynn show, *The Perfect Fool*, which opened at the George M. Cohan Theater on 7 November, ran for 256 performances. Gershwin had provided two numbers for it, one with lyrics by Irving Caesar — 'No One Else but That Girl of Mine' — and another by Caesar and Buddy De Sylva — 'My Log-Cabin Home'.

The next year, 1922, was somewhat unusual in that Gershwin had songs in two shows which opened on the same night, 20 February. The first was *The French Doll* at the Lyceum Theater, in which Irene Bordoni sang Gershwin's 'Do It Again' (lyrics by Buddy De Sylva), to great effect, and the second was *For Goodness Sake* at the Lyric Theater, which featured Fred and Adele Astaire and two Gershwin numbers, 'Someone' and 'Tra-La-La' — both to lyrics by Ira as Arthur Francis. Both ran for over 100 performances, the first 120 and the second 103. In July there was a show at the Winter Garden, *Spice of 1922*, to which Gershwin contributed

'Yankee Doodle Blues', which ran for seventy-three performances, and then it was on to the *George White's Scandals* of that year, which in addition to the *Blue Monday Blues* already mentioned, had a further nine Gershwin numbers. The *Scandals* opened on 28 August at the Globe Theater, and ran for eighty-eight performances. Of rather more than passing interest is the fact that W.C. Fields not only played in the show, but had a hand in the book as well.

For this show Gershwin provided one of his greatest early hits, 'I'll Build a Stairway to Paradise', to lyrics by both Buddy De Sylva and Ira (as Arthur Francis). It closed the first act, and Gershwin himself described its effect:

> I'll never forget the first time I heard Whiteman do it. Paul made my song live with a vigor that almost floored me . . . there was no stopping 'Stairway to Paradise' once Whiteman got his brasses into it. Two circular staircases surrounded the orchestra on the stage, leading high up into the theatrical paradise or flies, which in everyday language means the ceiling. Mr. White had draped fifty of his most beautiful girls in a black patent-leather material which brilliantly reflected the spotlights. A dance was staged in the song, and those girls didn't need much coaxing to do their stuff to the accompaniment of Whiteman's music.

Gershwin subsequently maintained that it was his association with Whiteman in this show that induced the latter to ask Gershwin to write the work that became *Rhapsody in Blue*.

The traffic was not all one way, however, for because Paul Whiteman, the 'King of Jazz', and his Palais Royal orchestra were featured in the 1922 *Scandals*, other inspiration flowed. Buddy De Sylva went to Gershwin with the idea of a Negro opera set in Harlem, and the pair of them then approached George White. Presumably it must have been the promised mixture of a drama of Negro life in Harlem, portrayed in jazz idiom, that won White over, for the projected length of twenty-five minutes is long within the timescale of any theatrical performance, let alone productions such as the *Scandals*. At all events, De Sylva and Gershwin finished *Blue Monday Blues* in five days, working round the clock. It was a failure.

Some of the responsibility for the failure certainly rests with the libretto, which is trite and naive. The three main characters are Vi, her lover Joe, who is a gambler, and the entertainer, Tom, who is

Joe's rival for Vi's affections. Joe receives a telegram to go and visit his old mother in Georgia, but he does not tell Vi because he does not want her to consider him a 'Momma's Boy'. Tom capitalizes on the situation by convincing Vi that Joe is leaving to visit another woman, which is of course true, but not in the way that Vi thinks. Vi shoots Joe.

The libretto evidently did not inspire Gershwin, and as a result the work consists largely of songs strung together with recitative. One of the best tunes, 'Has Anyone Seen Joe?', is taken from the string quartet *Lullaby*, but Gershwin failed to turn it into anything more than it had been in the beginning, which is a pity, because it has definite lyrical potential.

As if a poor libretto and indifferent music were not enough of a liability, the production certainly did not help either. For one thing, white actors were used and made to black up, so that any attempt at genuine realism failed dismally. Charles Darnton, reviewing the opera in the *World* after the first night at the Globe Theater on Broadway on 28 August 1922, declared that it was 'the most dismal, stupid and incredibly blackface sketch that has probably ever been perpetrated. In it a dusky soprano finally killed her gambling man. She should have shot all her associates the moment they appeared and then turned the pistol on herself.' Whether it was because of this reception or his own better judgement, White dropped it after the first performance. In his opinion, the tragic element of the opera threw the whole review off balance, and was in any case contrary to the general character of the *Scandals* as he saw them — namely, light-hearted entertainment for the widest possible public.

There was, however, one reviewer, who declared that: 'George White and his company have given us the first real American opera in the one-act piece called *Blue Monday Blues*. Here at last is a . . . human plot of American life, set to music in the popular vein, using jazz only at the right moments, the sentimental song, the Blues, and above all, a new and free ragtime recitative. True, there were crudities, but in it we see the first gleam of a new American musical art.'

There was also another reviewer who predicted: 'This opera will be imitated in a hundred years.'

Whatever the truth of the matter, Gershwin learned from the experience, and when he eventually came to try his hand again at a Negro opera with *Porgy and Bess*, he knew instinctively that

40

his work would have to be performed by black artists. In a purely musical context, Paul Whiteman, who conducted his orchestra for that memorable first performance, subsequently determined to give it another chance, and on 29 December 1925 gave a concert performance in the Carnegie Hall in a version orchestrated by Ferde Grofé (the original had been arranged by the Negro Will Vodery) and renamed *135th Street* (the café on which the action of the opera is centred was on the corner of 135th Street and Lennox Avenue). However, even on this occasion, when Gershwin's name was a household word after *Rhapsody in Blue* (1924), the work fared little better. Perhaps it ought to have been left in decent obscurity, and it is all too easy to forget, in the amazing development of Gershwin's reputation, that he was still only twenty-three when he wrote the original *Blue Monday Blues*, with virtually no formal training to do so.

There was one final Broadway show for Gershwin before the end of 1922, *Our Nell*, which opened at the Nora Bayes Theater on 4 December. This time Gershwin collaborated with the man who was probably his best friend, William Daly, with whom he had worked earlier in the year on *For Goodness Sake*. The show was not a success, and managed only forty performances, but it cemented the friendship between Gershwin and Daly.

In some ways the relationship between Gershwin and Daly was an attraction of opposites, Daly embodying many of the qualities that Gershwin aspired to. Eleven years older than Gershwin, Daly was a graduate of Harvard and an accomplished musician, able to compose, orchestrate and conduct. These skills alone were ones that Gershwin would have dearly loved to acquire as his career took off, but it went much deeper than that. Gershwin was self-made, had arrived with a bang, and intended staying on top. Daly, on the other hand, had to a certain extent been born to the part (though he had not devoted the whole of his career to music up to the time he began to collaborate with Gershwin). Daly was very relaxed, tended to think before he opened his mouth, and did not have to buy expensive clothes to impress or proclaim his success. He wore spectacles, too. Somehow one cannot imagine that Gershwin would ever have deigned to appear in public in spectacles, even if he had been as blind as a bat.

There was the touching, almost ingenuous trust in Daly, the college man, on the part of Gershwin, the Brooklyn boy, that one still encounters in some Pop musicians when they meet those trained in the traditional Classical way, whom they acknowledge to be 'legit.' in their own terminology. There was also the trust in the experience of the older man, especially when he did not constitute a threat to Gershwin's own sphere of activity. On the contrary, Daly was one of its most important props and stays, and the dedication to him of the three Gershwin piano preludes published in 1927 was a significant gesture on the composer's part. When, in August 1931, he wrote to George Pallay: 'I believe I have told you about Bill being probably my best friend', one cannot doubt Gershwin's sincerity, and the fact that he did not indulge in any great show of grief when Daly died, let alone commit himself to paper for public consumption, tends to confirm this. There can in any case be little doubt that Gershwin's friendship with Daly was one of the most satisfying he experienced, and possibly the most valuable, and was in sharp contrast to almost all of the composer's friendships with women.

A new Sigmund Romberg show entitled *The Dancing Girl*, produced by the Shuberts, opened at the Winter Garden Theater on 24 January 1923 and introduced yet another Gershwin–Irving Caesar song, 'That American Boy of Mine'. Then there were the *George White Scandals of 1923*, which opened in June, with a dozen Gershwin numbers, and in August *Little Miss Bluebeard* with one number. In September followed *Nifties of 1923* with two numbers, as well as a song to lyrics by Ira (Arthur Francis), 'The Sunshine Trail', to accompany a silent film of the same title. Even if there were no notable hits amongst any of this music, nevertheless it was all experience for the composer, and it all helped to keep his name before the public. Moreover, his fame was now spreading beyond America.

In the early part of 1923 George travelled abroad for the first time, to London, to write the score for a revue entitled *The Rainbow*, with lyrics by Clifford Grey. Gershwin had been offered a fee of $1,500, his return fare, as well as royalties from whatever songs from the show were published. But the opening night at the Empire Theatre on 3 April 1923 was not a success, and despite the rumpus caused by the leading comedian launching into an attack on favouritism being shown towards American actors in the revue, it is fair to say that Gershwin's music was not all that good. He returned to America rather with his tail between his legs.

By way of compensation, perhaps, later that year Gershwin enjoyed great acclaim as a result of a recital given by the Canadian soprano Eva Gauthier on 1 November (1923) at the Aeolian Hall in New York. There were five groups of songs in her 'Recital of Ancient and Modern Music for Voice', ranging from Byrd and Purcell to Bartók and Schoenberg, in which she was accompanied at the piano by Max Jaffe. For the sixth group, consisting of Irving Berlin, Jerome Kern, Walter Donaldson and George Gershwin, she was accompanied by the latter. It was a clever, not to say daring mixture for such a recital, but it cashed in on the fact that jazz was then very new in such a context, and therefore it was taken very seriously, especially when included in a programme of classical music.

One must bear in mind that polite American society had, in the closing years of the previous century, fought a rearguard action against the dissemination of jazz. The *Musical Leader* announced that 'the General Federation of Woman's Clubs has taken up the fight against jazz . . . the services of the *Ladies' Home Journal* have been enlisted . . . that form of music seems doomed'. Jazz was condemned as 'a meaningless stirabout, a commotion without repose, an epilepsy simulating muscular action', by one critic, who added, 'better than bad music is no music, and to let our beloved art subside finally under the clangor of subway gangs and automobile horns, dead but not dishonored'. What, one wonders, would he have made of the opening of the *Second Rhapsody* with its pounding rhythm, or *An American in Paris* with its taxi horns?

As late as 1918 the *Times-Picayune* of New Orleans attempted to disclaim any responsibility for jazz, which its editorial denounced in no uncertain terms. Its tunes, it said, were:

> manifestations of a low streak in man's tastes that has not yet some aid in civilization's work . . . jazz music is the indecent story syncopated and counterpointed . . . On certain natures, sound loud and meaningless has an exciting, almost an intoxicating effect, like crude colours and strong perfumes, the sight of flesh or the sadistic pleasure in blood. To such as these the jazz music is a delight and . . . gives a sensual delight more intense and different from the langour of a Viennese waltz.

If that were so, then America, quickly followed by Europe, was quite keen to embrace the new indecency.

Such sentiments help to put into context, however, just how daring the Gauthier concert of 1923 was at the time. Although many people had found that jazz was not turning them into crazed fiends, there were many concert-goers and lovers of classical music who would feel a certain frisson on learning that anything even faintly to do with jazz was going to be served up to them from the platform, and so the announcement of the recital programme ensured a good audience in advance.

It also ensured that the critics would be there, and so it gave Gershwin the opportunity to appear as both pianist and composer, and he stood up to the exposure very favourably. Deems Taylor wrote in the *World* that Gershwin, in his playing, did 'mysterious and fascinating rhythmic and contrapuntal stunts with the accompaniment'. The recital was repeated in Boston the following January, and Henry Taylor Parker*, writing in the *Evening Transcript* on 30 January 1924, noted how Gershwin had: 'diversified the songs with cross rhythms; woven them into a pliant and outspringing counterpoint; set in pauses and accents; sustained cadences; gave character to measures'. In short, Parker suggested that, as a composer, Gershwin marked 'the beginning of the age of sophisticated jazz'. Whereas the other popular composers had been represented by only one song each, Gershwin had had three — 'I'll build a Stairway to Paradise', 'Innocent Ingenue Baby' and 'Swanee', with 'Do It Again' as an encore.

Of course the whole concept of what was jazz and what was not was somewhat arbitrary at this time, and purists then and now knew perfectly well that much of what was served up — especially by the white musicians of the day — had little or nothing to do with jazz proper. Even so, as we have seen, people were aware that jazz had arrived, that things were changing and would never be quite the same again — not only in music, but in almost every domain of human experience — and in this widest of contexts, then it is true to say that the jazz age had dawned. Paul Whiteman, 'King of Jazz', in fact played very little jazz, but when he took on Ferde Grofé as pianist and arranger, between them they had created something that was not jazz, but was certainly new, good to dance to and to listen to, and highly successful. It was on the flood of this particular tide that Gershwin's *Rhapsody in Blue* was brought before the great American public and the world at large.

* He signed his reviews H. T. Parker.

44

3 RHAPSODY IN BLUE

Rhapsody in Blue

Whatever dreams for future compositions Gershwin might have had at any one time — and this applied virtually throughout his career — he almost always had to shelve them because of work in hand. Possibly the most notable example of this tendency was his long-held wish to write an opera on the Porgy and Bess story, once he had read the original book — a wish which had to wait several years before coming to fruition. With some composers this is a necessary and desirable process, for the work has time to mature in the musical mind before it is ready for articulation. Even then, for some composers the process of writing down is itself long and laborious, though there have been notable examples of others who were capable of seeing the music almost in its entirety in their minds and were then able to commit it to paper very quickly.

Rather like some musical journalists, Gershwin tended to need the stimulus of an approaching deadline before he began to write music, and then when he did, it all went very quickly, certainly in the earlier part of his career. In between bouts of composing, however, there is little evidence that he developed ideas or elaborated any conceptions. He did, of course, use existing material, but that was a different matter. Almost all his music was written at the keyboard, and was written down as it happened, so to speak, and indeed it seems as if this was virtually the only way that he was able to write. Later — in the Thirties — it seemed to provoke a genuine crisis, and drove him to seek professional help, for he found it extremely difficult to write down what he said he felt inside his head. In the hectic days of the early Twenties, however, this was not a problem, since Gershwin was so busy that it was almost as much as he could do to complete work in hand. A decade later, however, it would be a different story.

Luckily for Gershwin, other people turned ideas around, worked on them, and made positive plans for their execution. One such was Paul Whiteman, who was not deterred by what he had seen happen to the original version of *Blue Monday Blues* in 1922, and was convinced that it still had potential. Naturally he also felt that its composer had potential, too, and continued to watch his progress with interest. They had struck a friendship out of their working relationship during the 1922 *Scandals*, and remained in touch at this time, despite the fact that their careers were taking them both back and forth across the Atlantic, in opposite directions. Gershwin left for London first in 1923 for *The Rainbow*, and exactly a month before it was due to open, that is on 3 March, Paul Whiteman left New York on S.S. *President Harding* for an engagement at the London Hippodrome, and then returned to settle in at the Palais Royal on Broadway. As 1923 progressed, Whiteman decided that he would break new ground in New York, and take his jazz into the heart of establishment music, in the city's Aeolian Hall, where the Gauthier–Gershwin concert was such a success on 1 November that year. Indeed, its success probably gave added inspiration to Whiteman. Certainly he approached Gershwin and asked him to write a composition for piano and orchestra, and play the solo piano part himself. By the end of 1923, however, as far as Gershwin was concerned, the proposed work was still no more than a project.

Late on the evening of 3 January 1924, however, Gershwin was playing billiards with Buddy De Sylva when Ira Gershwin came in with an early copy of the following day's *New York Tribune*, in which it was reported that Gershwin was at work on a jazz concerto, the first performance of which was to be given by Paul Whiteman on Tuesday, 12 February. This in itself would have been enough to cause consternation, but it was also reported that there was to be a committee of judges who would 'pass on "What is American Music" ', and that their number would include 'Serge Rachmaninoff, Jascha Heifetz, Efrem Zimbalist and Alma Gluck'. Irving Berlin was said to be writing a 'syncopated tone poem', and Victor Herbert an American suite. In the event the Berlin contribution consisted of Grofé's arrangements — described as 'semi-symphonic' — of 'Alexander's Ragtime Band', 'A Pretty Girl is Like a Melody' and 'Orange Blossoms in California'. Herbert's *A Suite of Serenades* may merely have served to emphasize the cosmopolitan nature of America's inhabitants — if indeed the eventual suite was still meant to be 'American' as in the newspaper, for the serenades were — in order — Spanish, Chinese, Cuban and Oriental.

Despite the fact that Gershwin was still finishing off the score of a musical, *Sweet Little Devil*, which was scheduled to open at the Astor Theater in New York on 21 January, he began work on what was to become *Rhapsody in Blue* on 7 January, according to the title-page of the manuscript. Whiteman had suggested that Ferde Grofé should orchestrate the work as Gershwin composed it, which would undoubtedly save time, especially since, by now, Grofé knew the capabilities and resources of the band extremely well. Closely related to this fact is another piece of information from the manuscript — namely, that it was written for jazz band and piano. All too often the work is given with an orchestra of symphonic proportions, so that whatever the merits of this rendition from an aesthetic point of view, it nevertheless bears little relation to the original version, which we had an opportunity to hear during the Proms* in 1985, and which turned out to be closer to Kurt Weil in texture and timbre, especially with the mean-toned saxophones used on this occasion.

Olin Downes, in the *New York Times*, described the setting for the original concert, and at the same time gave a vivid impression of what those sonorities might have sounded like:

> Pianos in various stages of *déshabille* stood about amid a litter of every imaginable contraption of wind and percussion instruments. Two Chinese mandarins, surmounting pillars, looked down upon a scene that would have curdled the blood of a Stokowski or a Mengelberg.
>
> The golden sheen of brass instruments of lesser and greater dimensions was caught up by a gleaming gong and carried out by bright patches of an Oriental backdrop. There were also lying or hanging about frying-pans, large tin utensils, and a speaking trumpet later stuck into the end of a trombone — and what silky, silky, tone came from that accommodating instrument. This singular assemblage of things was more than once in some strange way to combine to evoke uncommon and fascinating sonorities.

* Promenade concerts – held annually in the Albert Hall, London, and conducted by Sir Henry Wood until his death.

Downes went on to admit that Gershwin was far from being master of his chosen form, but that the audience had been aware that here was 'a new talent finding its voice, and likely to say something personally and radically important to the world'.

By no means all of the reaction was favourable, however, and Lawrence Gilman wrote: 'Weep over the lifelessness of its melody and harmony, so derivative, so stale and so inexpressive. And then recall, for contrast, the rich inventiveness of the rhythms, the saliency and vividness of the orchestral colors.'

Much has been written since about *Rhapsody in Blue*. Constant Lambert pronounced that it was 'singularly inept . . . neither good jazz nor good Liszt, and in no sense of the word a good concerto'. Leonard Bernstein came to its defence and wrote: 'What's important is not what's wrong with the *Rhapsody*, but what's right with it. And what's right is that each of those inefficiently connected episodes is itself melodically inspired, harmonically truthful, rhythmically authentic.' It seemed that at one point early on, Gershwin had seen the work as an extended blues, but in the end decided on the form of a rhapsody which, if it means anything in musical terminology, indicates that it is in free form. But we have Gershwin's own thoughts on the matter, as conveyed by Isaac Goldberg in his *George Gershwin (1931)*; though since the style is rather more literary in tone than some of Gershwin's other utterances, one may be forgiven for suspecting that he was helpfully edited. Nevertheless, it is the composer, in element, who speaks:

> There had been so much chatter about the limitations of jazz, not to speak of the manifest misunderstandings of its function. Jazz, they said, had to be in strict time. It had to cling to dance rhythms. I resolved, if possible, to kill that misconception with one sturdy blow. Inspired by this aim, I set to work composing with unwonted rapidity. No set plan was in my mind — no structure to which my music would conform. The rhapsody, as you see, began as a purpose, not a plan.

Just as well, one might well add, since the very thing that Gershwin would have been incapable of doing was writing a work of regular, let alone traditional construction. But to say that is to judge the work by a set of values of questionable relevance. If the work succeeds on its own terms, then that is all that matters. Gershwin went on to relate how he had to go to Boston by train for the première of the pre-New York run of *Sweet Little Devil*, and how the construction of the rhapsody came to him, inspired by the insistent motion and noise of the train:

> No new themes came to me, but I worked on the thematic material already in my mind and tried to conceive the composition as a whole. I heard it as a sort of musical kaleidoscope of America — of our vast melting pot, of our unduplicated national pep, of our blues, our metropolitan madness. By the time I reached Boston I had a definite plot of the piece, as distinguished from its actual substance.

It would seem that Gershwin finished the composition of *Rhapsody in Blue* about 25 January, since Ferde Grofé took about ten days to score it, and he completed his task on 4 February, according to the date on his original score. Bearing on the composition of *Rhapsody in Blue*, much ink has also been spilt on the vexed question of who really orchestrated the piece — Gershwin or Grofé. From the available evidence, it would seem unlikely that Gershwin was capable of orchestrating the work at that point in his career, no matter what he or anyone else said, and indeed, it seems beyond doubt that it was Grofé who was responsible. What is more a matter for discussion is who orchestrated some of the subsequent works.

Gershwin made a great deal of money from *Rhapsody in Blue* — in fact, it has been estimated that in the first decade of its life he earned more than $250,000 from it. Whiteman, on the other hand, lost $7,000, although he repeated the concert on 7 March 1924, again at the Aeolian Hall, and then as a benefit for the American Academy in Rome on 21 April. The publicity — good or bad — that had surrounded the first concert, generated more interest, all of which has tended to put into the shade Gershwin's other activities in the early part of 1924.

To start with, there was the musical *Sweet Little Devil*, for which he had written no less than sixteen numbers, twelve of which were used in the final version of the show, which had opened on 21 January at the Astor Theater. Although there was not a hit song in it, it ran for 120 performances. Then there were the *George White's Scandals of 1924*, which opened on 30 June at the Apollo Theater and ran for 192 performances. All the songs were eventually published, though no doubt the best known was 'Somebody Loves Me'. That was the end of Gershwin's involvement with *Scandals*, however, though there was to be one last fling when *Rhapsody in Blue* was used as the finale to the first act of the 1927 *Scandals*.

As 1924 advanced, Gershwin prepared to return to London to write the score for another musical. This time, in marked contrast to the disappointment of *The Rainbow Revue* of 1923, the new show was a hit. *Primrose*, to a book by Guy Bolton and George Grossmith and lyrics by Desmond Carter and Ira Gershwin, opened at the Winter Garden Theatre on 11 September, with Heather Thatcher and Leslie Henson in the leading parts. For the first time, a vocal score of a Gershwin musical was published in its entirety, by Chappell in London and Harms in New York, though no one song from the show became a hit in its own right. What was perhaps more interesting from the point of view of Gershwin's development as a composer was the fact that he orchestrated some of the songs himself for the first time — according to Ira, 'a number or two'. There were in fact no less than eighteen numbers in the show, and although Gershwin drew on existing material for at least three of the songs, by far the majority were written especially for the show in London.

He stayed in a flat at 10 Berkeley Street, along with Alex Aarons and his wife, and it was from there on 8 July (1924) that he wrote to Emily and Lou Paley:

I am writing this small note to tell you how nice everything seems this year as compared with last. Alex Aarons, his wife and I have one of the cheeriest flats I've seen anywhere. It looks over Devonshire Gardens [the gardens of Devonshire House], and makes a comfortable place for me to work in.

Among the notables who have been in it since our invasion are Prince George [Duke of Kent], Otto Kahn, Lord Berners, The Earl of Lathom and several others.

The new show goes into rehearsal in two weeks. I hope to have it about finished by then. I am most optimistic about this show because the book seems so good — to say nothing of the score. We also have the best comedian in England to produce the laughter. If the show is only half-way decent it will be produced in America soon after its London presentation, which makes it doubly interesting.

The weather has been great — for London. It has been very cool.

He then went on to tell of some of the things that he had been doing when not working or mixing socially. He had seen the American player Hunter beaten at Wimbledon in a tough match, and he had played golf with Guy Bolton for only the eighth time in his life. He tied, and Bolton thought that he was a 'golf genius'. If he took it up professionally, that might be the way to 'knock off some heiress'. But certainly he found the atmosphere this time in London stimulating for his work, and he had not been there more than a week when he wrote the song called 'I'll Have a House in Berkeley Square, I'll Have a Cottage at Kew', which Aarons said was more English than any tune Paul Ruebens ever wrote, according to Gershwin. Perhaps that explained why, in the end, the show did not in fact transfer to America.

On the boat back to New York, Gershwin met Otto Kahn, and probably without very much persuasion played through to him some of the music for his next show, which he had already started in London. In particular he had with him 'Fascinating Rhythm' — or at least part of it — which Aarons, who was with him, had already earmarked for the show. Kahn was asked to put money into the show, but did not seem too interested until Gershwin played for him 'The Man I Love', which is said to have made up Kahn's mind at once, and he invested $10,000 in the production.

On returning to New York, Gershwin plunged into preparations for his next show, which was the Alex Aarons–Vinton Freedley production of *Lady, Be Good*, which was to mark another first, insofar as it was the first complete score that George and Ira Gershwin were commissioned to write together. The book was by Guy Bolton and Fred Thompson, and the cast was headed by Fred and Adele Astaire. As an additional attraction there was special scenery by Norman Bel Geddes, and from the musical point of view, an interesting addition to the pit orchestra of the two-piano team of Phil Ohman and Victor Arden. The combination worked so well that Gershwin used them again in *Tip-Toes, Oh, Kay!, Funny Face* and *Treasure Girl*.

In the show the Astaires played themselves, or rather a brother and sister dance team called Dick and Susan Trevors. They are having a hard time, however, at the start of the show, and since they are unable to pay their rent, they are thrown out onto the street with their goods and chattels. What follows is the way in which they try to win through and improve their lot. Dick decides to try and find a rich girl whom he can make up to for her money, and Susan decides to pretend to be a Mexican widow so as to inherit some money. Neither ploy works, but inevitably by the time the curtain falls at the end of the show, the Trevors have won through.

The show included a number of hits, among them, 'Oh, Lady, Be Good!', 'Fascinating Rhythm' — which Gershwin's father, Morris, always referred to as 'Fashion on the River' — and 'The Half of It, Dearie, Blues', though by one of those curious quirks of taste, one of the most famous of all Gershwin songs, originally destined for the score, never made it and was dropped before it opened in New York. 'The Man I Love' had been written during the spring of 1924, and was originally the introductory verse to another song. Gershwin then introduced it into the show, to be sung by Adele Astaire. When the trial-run started in Philadelphia on 17 November, however, it seemed out of keeping with the bright, brash atmosphere of the rest of the show, which was in any case on the long side, and since the audience did not warm to it, it was dropped after a week in Philadelphia.

And that might have been that, since Gershwin attempted to introduce the song into two more shows, but for various reasons it never made the grade, and yet it became, in its own right, one of the most famous Gershwin songs ever written, and achieved a popularity all of its own. The way in which it did so was an unusual one. Gershwin had by this time made the acquaintance of Lady Mountbatten, who asked Gershwin for an autographed copy of the song when she was in New York. He was pleased to comply, and she took the music back to London with her, and showed it to her favourite band, the Berkeley Square Orchestra. They played it, and since it was not in print, other bands played it by ear. It crossed the Channel to Paris, and then started coming back to America, but it was not really until 1928, when Max Dreyfus decided to publish and promote it, that the song really caught on in America.

So without 'The Man I Love', *Lady, Be Good* opened on 1 December 1924 at the Liberty Theater in New York, and ran for 184 performances. It was Gershwin's first undoubted smash-hit musical comedy, and it also served to confirm the reputation of the Astaires as a singing and dancing team. It later opened in London with three additional numbers, at the Empire Theatre on 14 April 1926, after a pre- West End two-week season in Liverpool.

Gershwin was now able to buy a five-storey house, 316 West One Hundred Third Street, which lies between West End Avenue and

Riverside Drive, into which the family now moved. George had the top floor to himself, whilst the second and third floors provided sleeping accommodation for the rest of the family, though when Ira married in 1926, he and his wife, Leonore, moved into the third floor. With a lift — in which Morris Gershwin loved to ride — to each floor, there was no problem over communications. The dining-room and living-room were on the first floor, and on the ground floor was a billiard-room that had once been a small ballroom. The Gershwins kept such an open house that when things got too noisy — even on the comparative isolation of the top floor — George got into the habit of decamping to the Whitehall Hotel some blocks away, where he took two rooms and could work in peace. In this way work went ahead for the music of 1925, which was once again to take Gershwin into the realms of 'serious' music.

Through the good offices of the conductor Walter Damrosch, in the spring of 1925, Gershwin was commissioned by Harry Harkness Flagler, president of the Symphony Society, to write a concerto for the New York Symphony Orchestra. Contracts were signed on 17 April, though not for the work itself, but for Gershwin to appear with the orchestra as a soloist in seven concerts between 3 December 1925 and 16 January 1926, performing the work which was referred to as *New York Concerto*. For the first two performances at Carnegie Hall on 3 and 4 December he was to receive $500, and thereafter $300 for each performance in Washington on 8 December, Baltimore on 9 December, Philadelphia on 10 December and Brooklyn on 16 January, but in the event the seventh concert never happened.

Before he got down to work on the concerto, however, Gershwin had other commitments. There was the Alex Aarons show *Tell Me More*, which opened at the Gaiety Theater on 13 April, 1925, but which ran for only thirty-two performances. The production fared better in London, where it opened on 26 May that year, once more with Heather Thatcher and Leslie Henson leading the cast. Gershwin went over to give a helping hand by writing one or two new numbers, and the show certainly did better business in London than it had in New York. He also managed to get over to Paris, according to a letter Ira wrote to the Paleys on 8 June (1925).

Whilst he was in London, Gershwin began sketching ideas for his new concerto, and by mid-July, when he was back in New York, he paid a visit to Edwin Knopf, and was already able to play him some of the themes. He began writing it down four days later on 22 July, since the writer and photographer Carl Van Vechten noted in his diary on 24 July that Gershwin had dined in his apartment that evening, and during the course of the meal told him that he had begun work on the concerto two days previously, and that he had already written five pages of it. Work seemed to go smoothly, either in George's own apartment, at his Steinway, or in the nearby Whitehall Hotel. At the end of July, however, and for most of August, Gershwin moved upstate to Chautauqua, where Australian born Ernest Hutcheson (1871–1951) gave master classes for piano. In this way, Gershwin could work in isolation if so wished, but also mingle with the students as a relief from work. On 20 July (1925) George Gershwin became the first American jazz musician to appear on the cover of *Time* magazine.

On the sketch for the concerto, Gershwin noted that the first movement was written in July, the second in August–September, and the third in September. Carl Van Vechten wrote in his diary that in October the work was finished all but for two bars, and then presumably Gershwin began the orchestration, which he completed on 10 November 1925. By this time the title of the work had changed from *New York Concerto* to *Concerto in F*. What remains a matter for conjecture is the extent to which Gershwin himself was responsible for the orchestration. In an article published in *Singing* (September 1926) the composer and critic A. Walter Kramer stated that he did not think that Gershwin, given his minimal technical equipment, was capable of having orchestrated the concerto. In reply, Gershwin wrote the following month in *Singing* that the work 'was orchestrated entirely by myself', and included page 70 of the score in his own hand. Even the most devoted Gershwin admirer is bound to admit, however, that one page of the score proves nothing in isolation. It is true to say that all the final scores in Gershwin's hand of the orchestral pieces that he composed after *Rhapsody in Blue* are in his hand, clearly written and orchestrated, but they give no indication at all as to what processes had to be gone through in order to arrive at these 'fair' copies. It is a question that will arise again in relation to *Porgy and Bess*, and one which will presumably continue to arise whenever the matter of Gershwin's orchestration is discussed.

When the work was complete, Gershwin took the Globe Theater and hired a sixty-strong orchestra at his own expense for a play-through. Walter Damrosch, who had commissioned the work, was also present, and it was doubtless at his suggestion, as well as that of Bill Daly, who seems to have — at the very least — made some observations on the instrumentation, that Gershwin made some quite extensive cuts in the work which were, by general consent, an improvement.

The première took place on the afternoon of 3 December in Carnegie Hall, and though the performance was a great success with the audience, the press were less enthusiastic, and the overall effect of the work was certainly less spectacular than that of the *Rhapsody in Blue* had been. In a way this was not surprising, since the circumstances were very difficult, but one cannot ignore the comments of critics such as Lawrence Gilman, who found the comments 'conventional, trite' and even, one has to say, 'a little dull'. Its significance lay more, one feels, in what it represented in the development of the Western tradition, and even more so of the American tradition, and so the words of Samuel Chotzinoff, another critic present at that first performance, who said, 'Of all those writing the music of today . . . he alone actually expresses us', take on considerable significance.

Gershwin himself published an account of the work in the *New York Herald — New York Tribune* of 29 November 1925, in which he made this point about the modernity and Americanism of the work:

> The first movement employs the Charleston rhythm. It is quick and pulsating, representing the young enthusiastic spirit of American life . . .
>
> The second movement has a poetic nocturnal tone. It utilizes the atmosphere of what has come to be referred to as the American blues, but in a purer form than that in which they are usually treated.
>
> The final movement reverts to the style of the first. It is an orgy of rhythms, starting violently and keeping to the same pace throughout.

Having said that, one wonders, as with many of Gershwin's public statements, how much was himself and how much was provided for him by someone else. For he is also on record as claiming that the concerto was in perfect form because it was in three movements. After all, he had admitted that he had bought 'four or five small books on musical structure to find out what the concerto form actually was.'

It took two years for the work to be heard in Europe, and then it was in Paris, at the Théâtre National de l'Opéra, in a concert conducted by Vladimir Golschmann on 29 May 1928, with Dimitri Tiomkin as soloist. By then its significance had come to lie in one aspect in particular that appealed to European musicians — such as Ravel, for example — and which was expressed by Walter Damrosch in somewhat florid terms:

> Lady Jazz, adorned with her intriguing rhythms, has danced her way around the world . . . But for all her travels and her sweeping popularity, she has encountered no knight who could lift her to a level that would enable her to be received as a respectable member in musical circles. George Gershwin seems to have accomplished this miracle. He has done it boldly by dressing this extremely independent and up-to-date young lady in the classic garb of a concerto. Yet he has not detracted one whit from her fascinating personality. He is the prince who has taken Cinderella by the hand and openly proclaimed her a princess to the astonished world.

As the year drew to its close, it must have seemed to Gershwin's friends — and rivals — that he had truly arrived on the New York music scene. After the première of the *Concerto* on 3 December, there was a lull of three weeks or so, and then, in quick succession, on 28 December the show *Tip-Toes* opened at the Liberty Theater; on 29 December Paul Whiteman gave the new version of *Blue Monday*, now *135th Street*, at Carnegie Hall; and on 30 December *Song of the Flame* opened at the Forty-fourth Street Theater.

Tip-Toes was another Aarons and Freedley production, and keen to repeat the success of *Lady, Be Good*, they once again turned for the book to Guy Bolton and Fred Thompson, and to George and Ira Gershwin for the music and lyrics. The Tip-Toes of the title is the dancer of a vaudeville trio, the Kayes. Tip-Toes herself was played by Queenie Smith, and her uncles Hen and Al Kaye by Harry Watson Jr. and Andrew Tombes. Marooned and broke in Palm Beach, the Kayes try to extricate themselves from their predicament by pretending to be members of high society. By plotting and scheming, Tip-Toes then meets and makes up to Steve, a young glue tycoon, played by Allen Kearns. But what started out as a piece of calculation on Tip-Toes' part turns serious when she discovers that she has truly fallen in love with Steve, and Steve realizes that Tip-Toes loves him for himself, and not just his money. So, after all, true love wins through.

Once again Gershwin used the piano duo Phil Ohman and Victor Arden, and among others in the cast was Jeanette MacDonald, as yet relatively unknown. Although there were no great hits in the show musically, it notched up 194 performances, and in fact the songs 'That Certain Feeling' and 'Sweet and Low-Down', both of which Gershwin published later in his own arrangment for piano solo, achieved continuing existence apart from the show.

The show *Song of the Flame* was a very different story. For one thing, Gershwin only collaborated on the music with Herbert Stothart, and Ira was not called in to provide lyrics. These were written by Otto Harbach and Oscar Hammerstein II, who also wrote the book. In many respects, nothing could be further removed from the atmosphere of *Tip-Toes* which, for all its predictability so far as its plot went, had a certain sophistication and charm. *Song of the Flame*, on the other hand, was ostensibly about a peasant revolt in Imperial Russia, but basically depended on the boy-meets-girl situation for its inspiration. It had a large cast, production numbers with lavish costumes and sets, dancers, and even the Russian Art Choir. Not surprisingly, in view of this, it ran for 219 performances, and so outran *Tip-Toes*, but alongside the more light-hearted musicals there was also a market for the exotic musical with its big production.

After the busy month of December 1925, the start of 1926 must have seemed rather dull for Gershwin, but he made another excursion into the world of more serious music when, on 8 February, he and the violinist Samuel Dushkin gave the first performance of *Short Story* at the University Club of New York. This was an arrangement by Gershwin and Dushkin from two piano pieces which Gershwin called 'Novelettes', one of which is dated 30 August 1923. One cannot claim that the end product as *Short Story* is any great credit to Gershwin as a composer, nor did the pieces come across any more successfully when he played them as part of a series at a concert given later with the contralto, Marguerite d'Alvarez (1892–1953), on 4 December, 1926, though the three preludes that he played on that occasion did subsequently establish themselves in the repertoire as the *Preludes for Piano*.

Whether or not Gershwin was disappointed with *Short Story*, he was able to plunge himself into the excitement of another trip to London, to prepare *Lady, Be Good* for its opening at the Empire Theatre on 14 April (1926), with a new number for the Astaires,

'I'd Rather Charleston', which reflected the continuing popularity of the dance, and the addition of the song 'Something About Love', which had first been used in *Lady in Red* (1919), as well as 'Buy a Little Button from Us', the new London opening number.

In between a visit to Liverpool for the pre-London try-out on 29 March and the London opening night, Gershwin decided to pay a visit to Paris, where he spent a week with Bob and Mabel Schirmer. Mabel, (née Pleshette) was a niece of the brothers Herman and Lou Paley. Lou's wife Emily was the sister of Ira's wife Leonore. This close-knit extension of the Gershwin family had from early days provided the brothers Gershwin with some of the cultural background and family ambiance that had been lacking in their own immediate home environment, and George remained closely attached to Mabel long after her marriage to Robert Schirmer. Indeed, he continued to depend on her, and her approbation in particular, as his career progressed. He felt able to confide in her in a way that seems to have been impossible with almost any other woman. Over and above the family ties, she had the musical background and, towards the end of Gershwin's life, she — like him — underwent analysis, and was aware of the problems it could create.

Bob Schirmer never seems to have been jealous of Gershwin's affection for his wife, and indeed their happy marriage appears to have been some sort of inspiration to the composer. Certainly the atmosphere of his visit to them in Paris in 1926 was in marked contrast to that of 1923 with Jules Galenzer, and it is no coincidence that it was a much more successful one from the artistic point of view, for it seems that Gershwin began to have inspiration at this time for another of his most famous compositions, *An American in Paris*, although he did not begin on it in earnest for another two years. According to Mabel Schirmer, he found the initial 'walking' theme fairly easily, but then he was stuck. He asked a somewhat mystified Mabel if they could go to the Avenue de la Grande Armée. In those days it was the place to buy automobile parts, and there Gershwin eventually found what he was looking for — taxi horns — to give him further inspiration. He took four of them back with him and used them in the completed *American in Paris*.

Bob and Mabel Schirmer accompanied Gershwin to London for the opening of *Lady, Be Good*, and Bob described both George's visit to Paris, and all three's trip to London, in a long letter to Emily and Lou Paley. In Paris they had taken George to a musical *Pas sur la*

Bouche, to give him some idea of what such shows were like there, but he left in the middle of the second act, saying that the bed at the Schirmers' house was more comfortable to sleep in than the seat at the theatre. Then there were visits to a boxing bout and the racecourse in the Bois de Boulogne, and an invitation to George Antheil and his wife to come to dinner. Antheil, described by Schirmer as 'that young super-radical composer', had tried to give Gershwin some idea of what his compositions were like, but since, according to Schirmer, most of his music was scored for 'sixteen grand-player-pianos, with an obligato by a boiler-factory', then it was not a very fair test. George, on the other hand, was not at all bashful about sitting down at the piano and giving excerpts from different things, such as show numbers, *Rhapsody in Blue* and the *Concerto*.

The subsequent visit to London when the Schirmers went back with George was memorable for several things, including a Paul Whiteman concert in the Albert Hall, during which Gershwin's hat and overcoat, which had been hanging up at the back of their box, were stolen. Then there was the first performance of *Rhapsody in Blue* done as a ballet in *The Midnight Follies* at the Hotel Metropole, and finally the opening night of *Lady, Be Good*, which was a triumph. They left the party after the show at about 2 a.m. but Gershwin was up until 8 a.m. There could have been no doubt about the show's success.

4 CREST OF THE WAVE

Crest of the Wave

In the days before Transatlantic air travel, crossing to Europe by boat was not only a very pleasant way — at least in theory — of getting there, but it invested the trip with considerable significance, and gave travellers much more time to adjust to their hoped-for destination. For Gershwin, Europe seems to have held remarkably little enigma as the place from where his parents had originated. True, as a child he had kept a scrapbook in which he pasted the pictures of 'Russian Musicians', as he titled them, but there was little overt curiosity about his Russian heritage in later years. No doubt the Revolution prevented any nostalgic hankering in any case, though there was one story, told by Rouben Mamoulian, when he was working with Gershwin on *Porgy and Bess*.

After a particularly exhausting morning's rehearsing, they had gone together to lunch at Lindy's — one of their favourite spots at that time — and unthinkingly Mamoulian had started humming a tune by Rimsky-Korsakov. Gershwin was so shocked that he turned to Mamoulian and said: 'Rouben, I think this is terrible! You have been rehearsing my music and here you are humming some Russian melodies. Why do you do that?' Mamoulian thought at first that Gershwin was joking, but soon realized that he was in deadly earnest. Besides, Gershwin was by then virtually incapable of that kind of humour. However, Mamoulian apologized, and although the lunch continued, Gershwin did not eat for quite some time. Eventually he began to smile, and triumphantly told Mamoulian: 'I know why you were humming that Russian music.' The rather wary Mamoulian asked why, and was told, 'Because my parents were Russian.'

The incident is really more instructive about Gershwin's

egocentricity as it developed, but it demonstrates that he really had little or no interest in Russia, and apart from the persecution of the Jews by Hitler, virtually no interest at all in Europe politically. From a musical point of view there was rather more incentive, especially when his musicals began to be put on in London, and then concerts of his music in various European capitals. Even so, there was not that looking to Europe, and at that time Paris in particular, as a source of creative inspiration that many other American composers, such as Aaron Copland and Virgil Thomson initially, had been seeking there from the beginning of the Twenties. But then, Gershwin had by now arrived.

Certainly it seemed as if Gershwin was riding on the crest of a wave in the spring of 1926 when he went back to America from Europe, and that was the time when Kay Swift recalled that she remembered him 'with much the most impact', though she had met him on previous occasions:

> He and his music were all of a piece — he was *exactly* like his music. And he had the face, personality, and the looks, and he moved exactly the way you'd expect from his music. I never saw anyone who was more like his music. As a matter of fact, I think people *are* like their work. I once met Ravel when he came over and wanted to meet Gershwin. He looked exactly like his music. You knew he'd written it.

Kay Swift had married the banker James P. Warburg in June 1918, when both of them were quite young, and had three daughters by him. The marriage lasted until 1934, when they divorced, though even by the time Kay met Gershwin in 1925, it seems to have been a relaxed enough arrangement for her husband not to object when an obvious friendship began to develop. Kay had many of the qualities in a woman that appealed to Gershwin. She was intelligent, witty, sophisticated, attractive — all the things he thought he looked for in a potential partner. Added to this was the fact that she was a musician in her own right, and had studied with Charles Martin Loeffler at the Institute of Musical Art. She was in fact a composer of no mean ability, and helped Gershwin to write down his music, correct his proofs or copy parts for him. She praised him in his success and supported him in adversity. As Gershwin dedicated the *Preludes for Piano* to Bill Daly, so he dedicated his *Song Book* to Kay Swift, thus acknowledging his considerable debt to both.

However, when it came to marriage, apparently Kay did not rate sufficiently highly for Gershwin. Perversely enough, her status as a divorcee, with three children, and the fact that she was not Jewish, all weighed against her. And doubtless, it must be admitted, Gershwin simply lost interest. Furthermore, would he ever have married anyone? Kay Swift destroyed all Gershwin's letters, and in 1939 married her second husband, a rodeo rider Chris Heyward, though she then divorced him and married a third time. She admitted that what ultimately defeated her as far as Gershwin was concerned was that she — in common with many women — wanted to be 'vitally necessary' to someone she loved, but to Gershwin she could never be that, however hard she tried. To her credit, she remained faithful to his memory. She prepared songs posthumously for publication in collaboration with Ira, and whatever her personal disappointment, she never went on record as having said anything adversely critical of Gershwin, other than expressing her personal regret at the fact that he never married her. She admired him as a composer and pianist. As she put it: 'George was somebody I'd rather hear play than anybody. He went right to the piano and sat down with joy.'

But there were some for whom the joy tended to evaporate when the playing went on for too long. There had been a time when Rose Gershwin warned her son against it, but he was irrepressible, and of course generally people were only too delighted to have him at their parties and willing to play. But it almost became a drug, and if he were not invited to play, then he would not trouble to conceal his disappointment. In response to his question to a friend whether his music would still be played one hundred years hence, Gershwin was given the answer that it would indeed, if he were there to play it.

Irving Caesar was also aware of this trait in Gershwin's character, though he saw more of a balance. On the one hand he found Gershwin 'very sweet and very soft and quite sensitive', which was by no means a side of him that many people saw, but on the other, he said that Gershwin had 'great faith and confidence in his music', and then went on: 'There was nothing modest about him. I don't mean that he was overbearing, but he had self-confidence, and rightly so. For when George sat down at the piano, there was no one who could move you as George would.' Caesar found it difficult to put his finger on Gershwin's talent, because of his involvement in what he called the 'serious field', but he was in no doubt that Gershwin had blazed a trail for all popular musicians, that his was a unique talent, and that he was in a class by himself — and is that not enough?

Gershwin was fêted by the rich and smart in New York society, and he attracted other talent as some kind of magnet. In 1926 he was confident, relaxed and to all appearances easy-going. Later, in less than ten years, in fact, he could be extremely touchy and difficult, and even devoted friends found it hard to know when they might not inadvertently cause him pain, as Mamoulian had found to his cost. It is a matter for regret that Gershwin was unable to build a relationship in these days of success, and in view of the happy endings of the shows he was writing at this time, it seems a bitter irony that he did not do so. Of course he might well have supposed that if he went on from 1926 in the same way, then no doubt he would find the right person and, like his musicals, marry and live happily ever after. So one cannot blame him for not grasping whatever opportunities that, with hindsight, one can see he had. And there were so many people, both from the days before his success and now with his new glory. Few people are on record as having declined an invitation to meet Gershwin, and more often than not they were falling over each other to get to him. As a measure of that success, people like Gertrude Lawrence were now beginning to acknowledge his talent and fame, and nothing succeeds like success.

Gershwin had known Gertrude Lawrence since 1924, when she made her Broadway debut in *André Charlot's Revue*, and when Gershwin was in England for *Lady, Be Good* in 1926, that friendship was strengthened. When Aarons and Freedley therefore approached her to appear in *Oh, Kay!*, she accepted without hesitation, and even, it was said, turned down an offer from Ziegfeld — also to appear on Broadway — in order to do so. She was to play Kay of the title of the show, though it started life as *Mayfair, Miss Mayfair*, then became *Cheerio*, before it ended up as *Oh, Kay!*

Born in London on 4 July 1902 as Gertrud Alexandra Dagma Lawrence Kasen, she rose to become 'the undisputed queen of the light comedy stage', and in many respects came to live the life of a queen as popularly envisaged. Yet there was dedication and professionalism, and of course pure talent, beneath her somewhat flamboyant exterior. As Noel Coward, who was probably associated with her in the mind of the public more than anyone else, has said:

> Her quality was . . . unique and her magic imperishable . . . there is no trick, mannerism, intonation, or turn of the head that I don't know by heart, and yet, watching her, as I have so often watched her, saying words that have not been written by me in scenes that I have not directed or even seen rehearsed, she has enslaved me.

With such a talent, then, as that of Gertrude Lawrence, the Gershwin musicals went on to reach a new peak with *Oh, Kay!*

The book, set in America during the Prohibition period, was by Guy Bolton and P.G. Wodehouse, and turned around the character of an English duke in straightened circumstances and his sister Kay. In order to recoup the situation, they attempt to bring bootlegged liquor into America on their yacht. Kay takes a job as a housemaid in the home of the wealthy playboy Jimmy Winter, whose cellar is used — without his knowledge, of course — to store the bootlegged liquor. Also employed by Jimmy Winter is Shorty McGee, the accomplice of Kay and her brother, whose task is to keep watch over the liquor. The whole adds up to a delightful mixture of comic mishaps mixed with the inevitable romance when Jimmy and Kay fall in love.

There were several memorable songs from the score, but perhaps the most typical as an example of the way in which George and Ira Gershwin worked together was 'Do, Do, Do'. The marriage between words and music is one of the best they ever achieved. Luckily Ira recorded the genesis of it in his *Lyrics on Several Occasions*:

> An hour so so before dinner one evening at our house on 103rd Street I told George that maybe we could do something with the sounds of 'do, do' and 'done, done'. We went up to his studio on the top floor and in half an hour wrote the refrain of the song. (I am certain of the time it took because just as we started to work, my bride-to-be telephoned that she *could* make it for dinner with us; and when she arrived, taxiing in half an hour — less, she says — from Eighth Street, we were able to play her a complete refrain.)

There were other good rhythmic numbers in the show, such as

'Clap Yo' Hands' and 'Fidgety Feet', but the show also contained the other kind of Gershwin song, the slow, romantic number, in this case 'Someone to Watch Over Me', which was sung in the show by Gertrude Lawrence to a rag doll. According to Percy Hammond in the *Herald Tribune* her rendition was sufficient to have 'wrung the withers of even the most hardhearted of those present' — though given the peculiar out-of-tune effect produced by Gertrude Lawrence's vocal timbre, that may not have been difficult.

Although Ira wrote most of the lyrics, he suffered an attack of appendicitis whilst work was going ahead, and had to spend six weeks in hospital, so Howard Dietz was called in to help. In this way, 'Someone to Watch Over Me' came to exist in the form we now know it. Apparently George had written the tune without any idea of lyrics or title, and as such it was rather fast and syncopated. In that form it would have been more likely to end up as a song-and-dance production number. However, one day Gershwin played it at a much slower speed, and he and Ira then realized that it would go much better as a slow, romantic number. When this version was played to Dietz, he suggested a number of alternative titles, one of which was 'Someone to Watch Over Me', and with this inspiration, Ira then wrote the lyrics it now has.

There was little doubt from the time that it opened in Philadelphia on 18 October 1926 that *Oh, Kay!* was going to be a resounding hit, and when it opened at the Imperial Theater on Broadway on 8 November, that impression was confirmed, and the show ran for 256 performances.

Not long after the opening of *Oh Kay!*, Gershwin appeared in the concert with Marguerite d'Alvarez already mentioned, which took place in the Hotel Roosevelt in New York on 4 December. Gershwin accompanied the singer in some of his songs — 'The Nashville Nightingale', 'Clap Yo' Hands' and 'Oh, Lady, Be Good' — as well as Jerome Kern's 'Babes in the Woods'. Then there were the piano preludes, consisting of the two 'novelettes' that made up *Short Story*, and the three later published as *Preludes for Piano*. More interesting, perhaps, and certainly more substantial an item on the programme, was the two-piano version of *Rhapsody in Blue*, in which Isidor Gorn played the second piano. The programme was repeated in Buffalo on 15 December, and in Boston on 16 January 1927, when Gershwin added a sixth prelude to his group of piano solos, which remained unpublished, and which Ira entitled 'Sleepless Nights' after his brother's death.

The Gershwin–D'Alvarez concerts never had anything like the success of the Gershwin–Gauthier recitals of 1923–4, partly because what had been different and exciting then lacked the novelty in 1926–7, and apart from the musically slight preludes, Gershwin was not offering very much that was new to his public. Indeed, it was Gershwin's name that prevented the whole enterprise from sinking without trace, for as it was, the concerts received very little coverage in the press. Possibly also, the period leading up to the opening of *Oh, Kay!* had so absorbed Gershwin's attention that he had not fully thought through the concert in advance, or he relied too much on what, by now, was already becoming his considerable reputation.

But it is too easy, given the Gershwin success story, to assume that he was always moving forward at this stage in his career. Despite his determination and considerable confidence in his own abilities, things did not always go his way. And in the light of his later glory, it is too easy to class as a disaster something which at the time was nothing of the sort — it simply did not fill the critics with enthusiasm. On the whole, though, Gershwin's career was moving forward, and already the seeds had been sown for what was to turn out to be one of his most remarkable products.

Early in October 1926, when Gershwin was deeply involved in rehearsals for *Oh, Kay!*, he took time one evening to read the novel *Porgy* by DuBose Heyward, which had been published in 1925 and become a best-seller. As Gershwin followed the story of Porgy and Bess he felt instinctively that it would translate to the theatre, and the musical theatre at that, and so wrote to Heyward suggesting that they might collaborate.

There are several points in the book at which Heyward particularly stressed the music of the area and its people: 'Instruments that glittered in the sunshine, launching daring and independent excursions into the realms of sound. Yet these improvisations returned always to the eternal boom, boom, boom of an underlying rhythm, and met with others in the sudden weaving and ravelling of amazing chords.' Then from the instruments he went on to the voices: 'singing drowsily, as though burdened by the oppression of the day. In another part of the building someone was picking a guitar monotonously, chord after chord, until the dark throbbed like an old wound.' From this it seems hardly a step to 'Summertime' as it eventually became in *Porgy and Bess*, and the whole atmosphere of Catfish Row in the opera as it evolved can be discerned in this: 'The rhythm swelled, and voices in the court and upper rooms took it up, until the deeply rooted old walls seemed to rock and surge with the sweep of it.' It would indeed have been strange if such vivid musical imagery did not speak to Gershwin directly. As it happened, Heyward's wife Dorothy began working on a stage version of the novel on her own, without telling her husband, and then they worked together on it for the Theatre Guild, which would have precluded any collaboration with Gershwin for some time. Writing to a friend in April 1925, Gershwin had already elaborated some thoughts about an opera with black characters and a black setting:

> An opera must be lyric, and to me it must be fantastic. I think it should be a Negro opera, almost a Negro *Scheherazade*. Negro, because it is not incongruous for a Negro to live jazz. It would not be absurd on the stage. The mood could change from ecstasy to lyricism plausibly, because the Negro has so much of both in his nature.

Eventually Gershwin and Heyward met, and Heyward recorded:

> We discussed *Porgy*. He said that it would not matter about the dramatic production (that the Heywards were doing for the Theatre Guild), as it would be a number of years before he would be prepared technically to compose an opera . . . And so we decided then that some day when we were both prepared we would do an operatic version of my simple Negro beggar of the Charleston streets.

There was no definite plan at this stage, however, but Gershwin was well advised to have staked his claim with Heyward, for when the play opened on Broadway on 10 September 1927 it was a great success and ran for 367 performances.

During the early part of 1927 Gershwin gave several performances of the *Concerto* which were fairly exhausting, and after which he went with Jules Glaenzer on a skiing trip to the Laurentian Mountains in Canada. By further way of contrast Gershwin then took a short holiday in Palm Beach, and in March again played the *Concerto*, this time with the Cincinnati Symphony under Fritz Reiner. The latter remained a Gershwin enthusiast, and after the composer's death, commissioned the orchestral synthesis of music from *Porgy and Bess* entitled *A Symphonic Picture* from Robert Russell Bennett, who wrote it during 1941 and 1942 for the Pittsburgh Symphony, which Reiner by now conducted, and with whom he gave the first performance in 1943.

In April 1927 the Gershwins rented a country estate, Chumleigh Farm, at Ossining in New York State, so that they could work in an atmosphere of calm on their next musical, and it was here that George Gershwin painted his first watercolour, towards the end of April. By contrast, Harry Ruby, who was one half of the Kalmar and Ruby songwriting team, brought a very different element to Chumleigh Farm when he visited it, since he was a baseball enthusiast, and did his best to get the others to join him. Only George could be induced to put on a glove and throw the ball for Ruby. Back in New York, they met in their publisher's office, and when they referred to the baseball episode, George acknowledged that Ruby threw very well. He could not prevent himself from adding, however, that he could also do well, were it not for the fact that he had to be very careful of his hands. He then added: 'With you it doesn't matter.' Ruby knew that Gershwin intended no personal insult, but it required great forbearance on the part of Gershwin's friends not to react to such remarks, which happened more frequently as time went by. When Ruby returned to the incident later at a Jules Glaenzer party, Gershwin had — true to form — totally forgotten it. Ruby recounted the whole story, and as he finished, Gershwin merely said, 'Well, it's true, isn't it?'

Oscar Levant had a fund of such stories, but one of the most telling was when he had to share a two-bunk sleeping compartment with Gershwin. As he took the top berth for himself without any hesitation, Gershwin merely remarked: 'Upper berth — lower berth. That's the difference between talent and genius.' For someone who needed people around him, Gershwin was remarkably indifferent to their feelings.

Ossining must have been a wonderful place to work, but short on company, so when rehearsals for *Strike up the Band* (as the next show was called) began in earnest in July, and the idea of commuting did not appeal, the Gershwins moved back into their city home. But the return facilitated plans for a concert at the Lewisohn Stadium in Manhattan, given on 26 July. It is estimated that on that occasion Gershwin performed before a crowd of 16,000–18,000 as soloist in both the *Rhapsody in Blue* and the *Concerto*, with members of the New

York Philharmonic conducted by Willem van Hoogstraten.

The reception given to Gershwin in New York on 26 July was in marked contrast to that given just over a month later to *Strike up the Band*, which opened at the Broadway Theater in Long Branch, New Jersey, on 29 August, and then at the Shubert Theater in Philadelphia on 5 September. After two weeks, the show closed, and never ever made it to New York. Opinions differ as to why the show failed, but if any one factor is to be held more responsible than the rest, it was probably George S. Kaufman's book that was simply too satirical, poking fun, as it did, at the way in which wars come about. There was a distinguished cast to put over Ira's lyrics and Gershwin's music, which included one of his most famous tunes, 'The Man I Love', but none of that could make the show, with its 'serious' message, appeal to the audiences. And doubtless it was ahead of its time. People wanted to go on believing that the First World War had indeed been the war to end wars, and in the freedom and affluence of the first decade after that war, a show that smacked of moral messages was not destined to be popular.

Potentially, *Strike Up the Band* was one of the more interesting books that the Gershwins had had to work on. Certainly if ingenuity of plot is anything to go by, it ought to have been a success on that score alone. The story turns on cheese. America has placed a fifty per cent tariff on Swiss cheese, and — not surprisingly, perhaps — Switzerland has protested. This so annoys Horace J. Fletcher, of the American Cheese Company of Connecticut, that he persuades Colonel Holmes of the White House to force Switzerland into war. Fletcher is perfectly happy to foot the bill for the war if America, out of gratitude, will name it the Horace J. Fletcher Memorial War. The cheese-maker has a daughter, called Joan, who is loved by a newspaper man Jim Townsend. With the help of a secret service agent, Townsend finds out that Fletcher is adulterating his cheese with Grade B milk. This so disgusts the reporter that he becomes a pacifist. In revenge, however, American patriots — who have already banned *Swiss Family Robinson* and *William Tell* from libraries and classrooms — discover that Townsend has a Swiss watch, and he is branded as un-American. When the war is declared, Townsend is called up, and Joan transfers her affections elsewhere.

The scene now moves to Switzerland for Act Two, where the war is going on. Whilst the noise of battle rages off stage, the troops are busy knitting for the poor folk in America. The Swiss hotels, in an attempt to encourage tourist trade, have offered competitive rates — even to American soldiers. Jim then indulges in a bout of yodelling, which enables the Americans to capture the Swiss Army. Then, as chance would have it, a Swiss spy is detected, and he confesses that it was he who adulterated Horace J. Fletcher's cheese with the Grade B milk. Jim now becomes a hero, despite the fact that he continues to protest that his views on the entire business have not altered. The Americans return home in triumph, being greeted with a great deal of praise, whilst at the same time losing their jobs. Peace is celebrated and the affair has turned out so well that when Russia now protests at the tariff on caviar, everyone agrees that she, too, must be taught a lesson, and the curtain falls to a reprise of 'Strike Up the Band'.

Reviewing the show after the opening in New Jersey, *Variety* said: 'That it will be a commercial smash is doubtful, but it will unquestionably have a *succes d'estime* . . . Satirical shows have never been a success in America, though the time may now be in sight.' *Variety* was not wrong, and although, after the Philadelphia opening, the *Inquirer* said: 'a rollicking show, a veritable geyser of spontaneous comedy . . . a thoroughly refreshing departure from routine', *Strike Up the Band* was doomed this time round.

When the show was revived in 1930, the war against Switzerland was reduced to a fantasy which only took place in the dreams of Horace J. Fletcher, and because it went so badly against him, when he woke up he was a reformed character. In addition, the cheese factory had been turned into a chocolate factory. Undoubtedly the show's pacifist message had been blunted almost to the point of invisibility, and some of the more perceptive critics felt that the original would have been better from that point of view. On the other hand, the revised version became a commercial success, and so far as the Gershwins themselves were concerned, it was that version which was much more pleasing.

Back in 1927, however, it seemed as if Gershwin had suddenly hit a bad patch, just when all had been going so well, for after the failure of *Strike Up the Band*, the next show, *Funny Face*, ran into terrible problems in its pre-Broadway run. The musical had been chosen by Aarons and Freedley to open their brand-new theatre on West Fifty-second Street which they had named the Alvin, taken from the first syllables of their respective first names, Alex and Vinton. It was crucially important for them that they should have a success to launch the new theatre, due to open on 22 November

1927. But despite the presence of the Astaires in the cast, and such well-tried ingredients as the piano duo of Phil Ohman and Victor Arden, when the show opened in Philadelphia, almost anything that might have been wrong with it seemed to be wrong — the book, the lyrics, the music, the singing, the dancing, even the casting.

The book, by Fred Thompson and Robert Benchley, and initially called *Smarty*, needed work doing to it, but Benchley withdrew and Paul Gerald Smith came in to help. It was hardly a complicated plot. Jimmy, to be played by Fred Astaire, holds some jewellery for his ward Frankie, played by Adele Astaire. Frankie and her boyfriend Peter (Allen Kearns) do their best to get hold of the jewellery, but so do a couple of incompetent would-be thieves. Out of such was the substance of the play made. However, Aarons and Freedley felt that the trouble lay principally not with the book, but with the music, and insisted on Gershwin's re-working it. He agreed, but they charged him some of the cost of the orchestration of the new score. It is estimated that the Gershwins dropped roughly half of the original songs and provided new ones whilst the show was being tried out in Philadelphia, Atlantic City, Washington and Wilmington. As Ira somewhat dryly observed: 'Everyone concerned with the show worked day and night, recasting, rewriting, rehearsing, recriminating — of rejoicing there was none.'

Almost incredibly, it seems — though it happened to the Gershwins before — one of the numbers which subsequently became famous, 'How Long Has This Been Going On', was dropped in the pre-Broadway run (though it was replaced with the successful 'He Loves and She Loves'). Even so, there were hits to make up for it, in particular ' 'S Wonderful'. By the time the show reached Broadway it had been transformed — into a hit. It reached the total of 244 performances, and in the first week alone, the box-office took $44,000. Paramount even considered turning it into a film the following year, and asked the Astaires to undergo screen tests. Somewhat surprisingly, in view of Fred Astaire's subsequent cinema career, it was felt that he was not suitable as a cinema star, and there, for the time being, the matter rested. It was not until 1957 — almost thirty years later — that Paramount finally got around to it! So far as Gershwin was concerned, however, it turned out to be no bad thing that so much material had been discarded from *Funny Face*, for before it was safely launched on Broadway, he had been drawn into another show, due to open within weeks of his own, but for the legendary Florenz Ziegfeld and the equally legendary Marilyn Miller. There was much at stake, but Gershwin accepted the challenge.

The show in question was *Rosalie*, which was due to open at the New Amsterdam Theater on 10 January 1928, and in theory the score ought to have been provided entirely by Sigmund Romberg. However, when it became clear that Romberg would be unable to finish on time, Gershwin was called in. Much of the material he eventually offered was either adapted from previous shows, or had been discarded from them. Of the seven eventually chosen for the new show, two songs came from *Funny Face*, 'How Long Has This Been Going On?' and 'Ev'rybody Knows I Love Somebody' — which in the original had been 'Dance Alone with You', but Ira provided new lyrics for *Rosalie* — and from *Oh, Kay!* came 'Show Me the Town'. Then there were some new songs, 'Oh Gee! Oh Joy!', 'Say So!', 'New York Serenade', and 'Let Me Be a Friend to You'.

The book was by Guy Bolton and Anthony McGuire, and the lyrics by P.G. Wodehouse and Ira Gershwin. The story — following on the visit of Queen Marie of Romania — concerns the visit of a princess from the kingdom of Romanza, who pays a visit to America and falls in love with an army lieutenant from West Point. The princess is obliged to return home, and the lieutenant flies across the Atlantic (the Lindbergh flight had taken place in 1927) to convince her of his love and claim her as his own. With Marilyn Miller as the princess, the show ran for 335 performances, and was to lead to further collaboration between Gershwin and Ziegfeld.

With *Rosalie* successfully launched on Broadway, Gershwin once again turned to orchestral composition and this time to *An American in Paris*. He had been to Paris in April 1923 after the débâcle of *The Rainbow Revue* in London that year, and again in 1925 and 1926. True, he had made a promise to Walter Damrosch that he would write a piece with the conductor in mind, but that would not specifically point to this. What seems more likely is that he had already decided on a trip to Europe, and beginning *An American in Paris* in January may have been a way of consolidating his endeavours, for on 18 February he gave an interview to *Musical America* in which he said that he was sailing for Europe in March, taking in both London and Paris. Whilst he was abroad, he would be working on an orchestral ballet entitled *An American in Paris*, and that he also intended to study. The information was repeated in the

New York Times on 9 March, but by then there was much more point to it, since on 7 March, at a party given by Eva Gauthier that evening to celebrate the fifty-third birthday of Maurice Ravel, Gershwin — at Ravel's request — met the French composer, and determined to meet him again when he reached France. On 11 March, George and Ira, their sister Frances and Ira's wife Leonore, left New York.

5 AN AMERICAN IN PARIS

An American in Paris

T here is a saying, attributed to Thomas Appleton (1812–84) though elaborated subsequently by Oscar Wilde in *A Woman of No Importance*, to the effect that good Americans, when they die, go to Paris. That may well have been so in the nineteenth century, but in the twentieth they declined to wait so long, and decided to go there during their own lifetimes. After all, why wait so long for all the fun. Of course Paris meant very different things to different people. From an artistic point of view, however, there was little doubt that virtually all that was happening of interest was happening in Paris.

In the realm of music, for example, there was much to be said in its favour at this time, for as far as some were concerned, Debussy's *Pelléas et Mélisande* (1902) had been the window through which the light of the new century had poured in. If there was any doubt about that, then there can have been little doubt about the significance of the shattering première of Stravinsky's *Le Sacre du Printemps* in 1913. By 1921 the boats were loading up with Americans coming to imbibe at the source, and yet the muse had departed long since, had the truth be known. With her usual perception, Gertrude Stein, in *Paris France* — though written much later — put her finger on that curious fact:

What made Paris and France the natural background of the art and literature of the twentieth century. Their tradition kept them from changing and yet they naturally saw things as they were, and accepted life as it is, and mixed things up without any reason at the same time. Foreigners were not romantic to them, they were just facts, nothing was sentimental, they were just there, and strangely enough it did not make them make the art and literature of the twentieth century but it made them be the inevitable background for it.

Paris drew people to it with a magnetic force, and few remained immune to its attraction. The fact that that attraction remained so potent for so long is only partially explained by Gertrude Stein, for it was something of a two-way affair. Although Paris no longer had the creative force it had once had, many of those who came to live there did not really care — if and when they became aware of the fact — and so it was in everyone's interests to keep up the illusion, much as Venice had been kept alive in the eighteenth century, because it suited many different purposes to do so. Then one day Napoleon arrived, and it was all over; though in the case of Venice, too, the artistic illusion lingered on, and for some still does.

Gershwin was remarkably free from illusions about people or places, and there is absolutely no evidence that he was bewitched by Paris. There is, however, a story that, on his first visit to Paris in 1923, as he rode through the city in a cab, he was moved to observe to his companion, Buddy De Sylva: 'Why, this is a city you can write about!' To which De Sylva is said to have replied: 'Don't look now, George, but it's been done.' Of course Gershwin did not have a great reputation as a bibliophile, and when he agreed to appear in an advertisement for a well-known house with the slogan: 'I am never bored by a Borzoi book', his friends duly remarked: 'Obviously he couldn't be bored with books, he never reads any.' He did, however, read *Porgy*, much to our benefit. Whilst one might deplore Gershwin's lack of what was once regarded as a basic education — and of course it was sad that he missed so much that European culture had to offer him — at least the lack of it enabled him to respond directly to stimuli as they touched him, and there was something refreshing and reassuring about his naiveté, as there still can be in Americans in their first encounter with new experiences. If any foreign city seems to have made an impression on him, it was London, rather than Paris. The fact that he wrote a piece of music entitled *An American in Paris*, therefore, had very little to do with the impression the city made on him, and a great deal with how he saw it, from an American point of view. He was remarkably free from any nostalgic longing for the past, and when he said 'my time is today', that was correct.

So far as the more perceptive of those close to him were

concerned — though it must be confessed that they were few and far between — this apparent inability of Gershwin's to be affected to any appreciable degree by anything outside him amounted to a kind of emotional immaturity, or arrested development, and in their eyes it led him to indulge in ready-made musical emotion, which did not augur well for the future. By this time, however, (early 1928), he had created his own momentum, which was carrying him along in a triumphal progress.

On 24 March, Gershwin saw Gertrude Lawrence in the last performance of the London run of *Oh, Kay!*, which had opened at His Majesty's Theatre on 21 September of the previous year (1927). The next day he was in Paris, installed at the Majestic Hotel, where he was to write the blues section of *An American in Paris*. The list of names of musicians Gershwin met in Paris is indeed imposing — Georges Auric, Nadia Boulanger, Jacques Ibert, Darius Milhaud, Francis Poulenc, Serge Prokofiev, Maurice Ravel, Vittorio Rieti, Leopold Stokowski and William Walton. Many were friendly, but some, like Prokofiev, doubted whether Gershwin really had the potential to become a serious composer.

His music was being performed, though a version of *Rhapsody in Blue* at the Théâtre Mogador on 31 March appalled him, it was so bad. The orchestra on that occasion was the Pasdeloup, which Vernon Duke described as: 'a worse than mediocre Paris orchestra whose idea of jazz was the *Folies Bergère*'. And Ira recalled: 'I alternately giggled and squirmed during this performance. It was at times almost unbelievably bad.' Nevertheless the piece was rapturously received, and there is an interesting aspect in that, according to Ira, it was the jazz band arrangement that was used, and not one of the more heavily orchestrated ones. Gershwin had found it all so excruciating, however, that he had taken himself off to the bar, to meet the others after it was all over. It came as a surprise to him, then, to have to go onto the stage in order to take a bow.

A more artistically satisfying evening was the one they attended on 16 April (1928) at the Théâtre des Champs-Elysées — which Ira said was one of the loveliest theatres he had ever seen, and which had much more charm than the Ziegfeld — when Anton Dolin and the Ballets Russes gave a choreographed version of *Rhapsody in Blue*. Dolin himself represented jazz in this version, Vera Nemchinova Classical Music, and the substance of the ballet was a contest between the two.

83

As well as writing music, Gershwin had let it be known that he was also looking for a teacher whilst he was in Paris, though one wonders how much time he would have been able to devote to lessons, in view of the way he spent his days. Certainly he worked at his composition. It was notable, however, that when Ira and Leonore, Frankie and Leopold Godowsky went to the Louvre, George went shopping. And in the event, nothing came of the idea of having music lessons, though much has been written about Gershwin's attempt to have lessons with Ravel and Nadia Boulanger, for example, and it is difficult to disentangle fact from fiction. According to Eva Gauthier's version, Ravel is supposed to have told Gershwin that if he were to study with him he 'would probably cause him to write bad Ravel and lose his great gift of melody and spontaneity'. Nadia Boulanger is reported as having said much the same thing, but she was an adroit person, and it would have been strange for her to have taken Gershwin on, knowing that Ravel had declined. Although she denied that she doubted Gershwin's ability to cope with an intense course of traditional classical study of the sort she administered, one feels that the fact remains that he simply would not have been able to respond to that aspect of her teaching. Elsewhere she is reported as saying that: 'It is never wise to enter a tunnel unless there is a good chance of coming out on the other side' — which fits in well with what one knows of her methods and some of her less than successful relationships with certain would-be pupils. Less robust characters than Gershwin found the contact with Nadia Boulanger too devastating, but one presumes that he would simply have gone away if they had not got on.

On 22 April, Gershwin went from Paris to Berlin, where he met Kurt Weill on the 24th and had lunch with Franz Lehar the next day. Then two days later it was on to Vienna, where the party was met by Emmerich Kálmán, who took them to a grand lunch at Sacher's where the band played *Rhapsody in Blue* in honour of its composer. On 29 April Gershwin attended a performance of Krenek's jazz opera *Jonny Spielt Auf*; then, on 3 May, he went to lunch with Lehar, who had also come on to Vienna from Berlin, and that same day Gershwin met Alban Berg. One of Gershwin's treasured possessions was a photograph of the latter, inscribed and decorated with a quotation from the Lyric Suite. It is dated 5 May, the day on which Gershwin attended a performance of Berg's string quartet — according to Ira. It seems, in retrospect, that there were some curious juxtapositions on that European trip — Weill and

Lehar in Berlin, Kálmán and Berg in Vienna — but such was the openness of the majority of the composers at the time, at least on a social plane. Even so, it is perhaps more surprising for Berg to be included in the same breath as Gershwin. The latter found he had a genuine and spontaneous affinity with Berg, to the point that he brought back an autographed copy of the Lyric Suite (in the string quartet version), which became a highly treasured possession. Gershwin's comments — as reported in *Musical America* of 18 August 1928, on his return — seem, in retrospect, staggeringly patronising: 'One of the high spots of my visit was my meeting with Alban Berg . . . Although this quartet is dissonant . . . it seems to me that the work has genuine merit. Its conception and treatment are thoroughly modern in the best sense of the word.'

On 6 May, Gershwin was back in Paris, for Cole Porter was putting on a show, *La Revue des Ambassadeurs,* and Frankie Gershwin was engaged to sing in it at a salary of $200 per week. This had all been arranged very much at short notice, before the Gershwins left for Berlin, and as a result she had to stay behind and did not go to either Berlin or Vienna. George had agreed to accompany her at the piano on the opening night, arranged for 10 May, with a gala performance and audience. In fact George did not really approve of Frankie's choice of a singing career, and in agreeing to help her in this way — according to Ira — he was somewhat going against his better judgement.

Frankie's singing career was not something that suddenly developed overnight. At the tender age of ten she had sung in public, and Ira recalled going to see her on 6 May 1917, along with George, at a recital given by her school at the Terrace Gardens on 58th Street. The next day Rose Gershwin took her daughter for a week's engagement in Philadelphia, and later that month she joined the show *Daintyland* at a salary of $40 a week, which was much more than either of her musical-oriented brothers was to earn for some time to come. In fact the money was more than enough to provide for Frankie and her mother whilst they were on the road. According to Frankie's own account, her mother did little to educate or bring up her daughter, and she always maintained that she brought herself up. Of course her marriage to Leopold Godowsky Jr. who, with Leopold Mannes, invented the Kodachrome process as used in colour photography, eliminated financial worry once and for all, and from that point of view, her Paris appearances were more of a swan-song than an artistic debut.

Ira was not actually present for the opening of the show, since he and Leonore had gone on to Budapest from Vienna, where she was taken ill. They did not finally return to Paris until 22 May, by which time Frankie was no longer in the show, since she and some of the other performers were so appalled by the noise from the kitchen and waiting staff, and no doubt diners as well, that they had decided to withdraw. George, however, had been working away at *An American in Paris*, and was being bombarded with missives from Walter Damrosch.

Damrosch had only heard that Gershwin had arrived in Paris by 4 May — by which time the composer was in Vienna — and wrote to invite him to lunch the following day — Saturday, 5 May — but Gershwin did not arrive in Paris until Sunday, 6 May. On Tuesday, 8 May, Damrosch was due to leave for Marienbad. In his letter he said that he would love to arrange to perform Gershwin's new work — *An American in Paris* — with the Philharmonic in the course of the ensuing winter season, and that he was practising the *Concerto* in the meantime. When he discovered that Gershwin was still in Vienna, he sent a cable the next day, but it was not until three months later, when both men were back in America, that Damrosch began to get some positive reaction from Gershwin.

Meanwhile, the European première of the *Concerto* was given at the Paris Opéra on 29 May, conducted by Vladimir Golschmann and with Dimitri Tiomkin as soloist. Writing in the *Christian Science Monitor* on 7 July, Emile Vuillermoz declared:

> Gershwin's concerto will greatly help to dissipate the last prejudices attaching to the new technique that has emerged from the novelties of jazz . . . This very characteristic work made even the most distrustful musician realize that jazz, after having renewed the technique of dancing, might perfectly well exert a deep and beneficent influence in the most exalted spheres. There is, in this mixture of balance and suppleness, a whole series of indications from which the most serious music might reap advantage.

The way in which Europe took Gershwin seriously at this time is a fascinating illustration of what is one's ultimate conclusion, that he offered a new stimulus and point of departure to many European composers by his very existence, rather than because of the inherent quality of his work.

The programme for that Paris Opéra concert began with Weber's *Euryanthe* overture, then Tiomkin played the Liszt Second Piano Concerto, followed by Copland's *Cortège macabre*, for orchestra, and then finally came the Gershwin piano concerto. The inclusion of the Copland piece is an interesting comment on the relative standing of the two composers then and now. Copland had studied with Boulanger in Paris from 1921 until 1924, and in the following year she had been the soloist in the first performance of Copland's Symphony for Organ and Orchestra with the Boston Symphony Orchestra under Walter Damrosch. In 1928, however, on the poster for the Gershwin concert, the latter's name is in print twice the size of the other composers, and Copland is misspelled as 'Copeland'.

It must have been something of an irony for Boulanger to attend one of the parties given for the Gershwins in the wake of that concert — one in particular at which Ira had noted her presence was given by Mrs Byfield at 179 Rue de la Pompe — and one wonders how that ascetic figure related to what Ira described as 'a mixture of Mayfair, the Rialto and Left Bank'. More immediately she had seen the work of one of her pupils, Copland, eclipsed by a man whom she had declined to try and teach, but whose ability as a composer — we may conclude — she did not rate highly. She was, however, well connected, and very socially minded almost to the end of her long life, and she did much to try and promote the work of her American students in the Twenties. She was also half Russian, of course, and must have known something of Gershwin's origins, though her descent was considerably more aristocratic than his. Moreover, she had always maintained that musicians had to try and assimilate the avant-garde works of any particular epoch, though her adored Stravinsky seriously embarrassed her when he embraced dodecaphony*, a discipline against which she had consistently set her face until then. One cannot pretend that she saw Gershwin as anything comparable to the Viennese School and their disciples, but if she were to remain true to herself then she would have to have accepted that he represented at least part of the new music. With her rigorous classical training, however, one suspects that she would have found much in the *Concerto* to criticize unfavourably, had it been set before her as a student's work.

---

* System of composition with 12 notes of equal status.

Indeed, there must have been several compositions that she would have preferred to see on that concert programme alongside her former pupil Copland.

Vernon Duke had taken Diaghilev and Prokofiev to the concert, but the former — according to Duke — shook his head and muttered something to the effect that it was 'good jazz and bad Liszt'. Prokofiev, however, was somewhat more well disposed towards Gershwin, and asked Duke to bring him to his apartment the following day, since he had been intrigued by some of the pianistic invention evinced in the work. Gershwin, only too delighted to display his talents, as usual, went and 'played his head off'. Prokofiev liked the tunes and Gershwin's embellishments of them, but did not think very much of the *Concerto*, which the composer played through to him. Later Prokofiev told Duke that he thought the *Concerto* consisted merely of 32-bar choruses ineptly bridged together. Nevertheless, the overall opinion of Prokofiev was that Gershwin was gifted both as a composer and a pianist, and he thought that he would go far if he left 'dollars and dinners' alone.

There had been several dinners, and plenty of parties, in Paris at this time, but the European holiday had to end sooner or later, and on 3 June Gershwin began packing up in Paris for the first leg of his return journey to America, which was to take him to London. In London he was to discuss with Alex Aarons and Gertrude Lawrence a new show — *Treasure Girl* — which was due to open in New York in November (1928), so Leonore and Ira remained in Paris, and met George at Southampton on 13 June. Five days later they were back in New York. Gershwin, fêted in European capitals as America's leading young composer, now had to get down to some very hard work, for in America he had to provide some evidence that his talent was as fresh and as vital as ever.

Soon, however, some indication of the fact was given to the American public, when it was reported in the *New York Times* of 6 June 1928 that the Philharmonic would give the first performance of Gershwin's new work — *An American in Paris* — in the course of the ensuing season. Two weeks later the same paper reported that the Gershwins had returned to New York, and no doubt the new work was high on George's list of priorities, but at the same time he had to finish the next Aarons and Freedley production, to star Gertrude Lawrence, which was due to open on Broadway that autumn. The new show was to be *Treasure Girl*, but there was also a projected Ziegfeld show, *East is West*, though in the end this was never produced. It must have seemed to Gershwin, once he was back in the thick of his New York existence, that Europe, and Paris in particular, was very far away, and indeed he never travelled there again.

Whilst he had been in Paris earlier in 1928, Gershwin had had a cable from Ziegfeld, asking him to write the music for a new Eddie Cantor show to begin rehearsals in September. Ziegfeld may already have known of Gershwin's previous commitment to *Treasure Girl*, for in his cable he asked that if the composer were not able to take on the Eddie Cantor show, would he write the music at least for one show for Ziegfeld. When Gershwin returned to New York, Ziegfeld then produced the idea of an adaptation of the play *East is West**, which was to star Marilyn Miller and Ed Wynn, and have a much closer relation between book and plot than was usual on Broadway. Gershwin agreed, and he and Ira started work on the show, without even having a contract, during the summer of 1928. It was not until the following year that they realized that Ziegfeld was not going to do the show after all, though of course the music was not wasted, and reappeared later in other forms.

Nevertheless, *East is West* took third place in preference to *Treasure Girl* and *An American in Paris*, both of which were due to be heard first within a month of each other in the latter part of 1928. The musical was not a success. It opened in Philadelphia at the Shubert Theater on 15 October, and then on 8 November at the Alvin in New York, but failed to find a favourable press and so closed after only sixty-eight performances. Not even Gertrude Lawrence's presence could save the show, and indeed, the role she had to play was that of a far from attractive woman — according to Ira — which confused and dismayed her public. Luckily, perhaps, for Gershwin, there was not much time for regret, since *An American in Paris* was now definitely programmed before the end of the year.

Damrosch had naturally been anxious to find out what exactly Gershwin was going to offer him for the new work, and on 5 August (1928) wrote to the composer, inviting him to visit him at Bar Harbor in Maine to discuss progress. Gershwin was able to report:

> I am glad to report that I have finished the sketch of *An American in Paris*; and in a day or two will have finished a two piano arrangement. The next move, of course, is the orchestration.

* by Samuel Shipman and John Bittymer.

89

Besides this I have the new Gertrude Lawrence show to finish. That goes into rehearsal in three weeks. With all this work you can see that it is difficult for me to designate the time when I can visit you. However, at the first opportunity that presents itself I shall wend my way Bar Harborwards.

To this somewhat tetchy response, Damrosch replied on 21 August with urbanity: 'Just a line to tell you that I am beset by numerous charming and altogether exquisite young creatures with "Is Mr Gershwin coming to stay with you", "When is Mr Gershwin coming", "Wonderful" . . . So please do not forget your promise and of course bring the score, finished or unfinished, of *An American in Paris* with you.'

In the event Damrosch was eminently forbearing, for by the beginning of November he still had not seen the orchestrated score and was beginning to be rather anxious. So on 5 November he wrote to Gershwin to tell him that the work had now definitely been scheduled for 13 and 14 December, and that he was consequently eager to hear the score as soon as possible. He also wanted to know how long the work lasted, so that they could plan the rest of the programme. He tried to conceal his anxiety in a polite invitation: 'Couldn't you come in some morning and play it over for me so that I can get your tempi and the proper spirit. If you could come for luncheon, not only I, but my wife, would be doubly pleased. How about some day next week?'

Had Damrosch been aware that Gershwin had barely completed the orchestration at that point, he may well have felt it necessary to postpone the projected première, for according to Gershwin's own annotation, the preliminary sketch had been completed on 1 August, and the orchestration on 18 November, both 1928. As early as mid-August, however, Gershwin gave an interview to *Musical America*, and was quoted at length in the issue of 18 August, talking of *An American in Paris* as something already complete in its conception:

This new piece, really a rhapsodic ballet, is written very freely and is the most modern music I've yet attempted. The opening part will be developed in typical French style, in the manner of Debussy and the Six, though the tunes are all original. My purpose here is to portray the impressions of an American visitor in Paris as he strolls about the city, listens to the various street noises, and absorbs the French atmosphere.

As in my other orchestral compositions, I've not endeavoured to present any definite scenes in this music. The rhapsody is programmatic only in a general impressionistic way, so that the individual listener can read into the music such episodes as his imagination pictures for him.

Such specific claims invite a certain number of observations. Although Gershwin had returned from Paris with the complete works of Debussy in eight leather-bound volumes, one would be hard put to point to anything in *An American in Paris* that has any stylistic similarities between it and the music of either Debussy or Les Six — though he may be forgiven for lumping them together, and it seems to be gnat-straining to point out that there were considerable differences between Debussy and Les Six. Satie might have been as apposite, but to an American, brought up largely in the mainstream of popular music, it would have been very difficult to distinguish between them without considerable study. One wonders how much of the music of Les Six Gershwin had even heard at this point.

Then there is the matter of there being no 'definite scenes' in the music. By the time it received its first performance with the New York Philharmonic under Walter Damrosch at Carnegie Hall on 13 December 1928, Gershwin had prepared with Deems Taylor a detailed programme for the work which was printed with the programme notes for the concert. On the other hand, from 'rhapsody' and 'programmatic' the work had been turned into a 'tone poem for orchestra' by the time of its first performance, so that what was added in the way of programmatic content was to some extent counteracted by the vagueness of 'tone poem'. But insofar as there was no solo piano in the work — and this was Gershwin's first major work to do without one — then the term 'tone poem' was probably justly applied.

Once again, however, the question of orchestration arose. Had Gershwin done it all himself? Four years after its première, when Gershwin himself conducted a performance on 1 November (1932) at the Metropolitan Opera House, one of the viola players, Allan Lincoln Langley, noted that the composer was so dependent on William Daly during rehearsals, that in the December edition of *The American Spectator* Langley wrote: 'The genial Daly was constantly in rehearsal attendance, both as *répétiteur* and advisor, and

91

any member of the orchestra could testify that he knew far more about the score than Gershwin.' Langley referred to 'blatant orchestrations' and 'transparent anachronisms' in Gershwin's serious music, and concluded: 'The point is that no previous claimant of honors in symphonic compositions has ever presented so much argument and controversy as to whether his work was his own or not.'

In fact, according to some sources, the key moment came not during the playing over of *An American in Paris*, but during the rehearsal of a group of four Gershwin songs for which Daly had written connecting transitional passages, as well as orchestrating the whole group. When a trumpeter played a certain passage during one of the transitional sections, Daly seemed surprised and asked: 'Did I write that there?' It was on the strength of this, then, and his personal experience of the rehearsals in general, that Langley asked himself how it was that Gershwin could have written and orchestrated all his own work.

Gershwin made no public statement, but Daly turned to the defence, and a letter appeared in the *New York Times* on 15 January 1933. He took the bull by the horns and wrote: 'Langley definitely tried to convey to the reader the idea that Gershwin is not the orchestrator, and probably not the author, of the works attributed to him.' Whether Langley had in fact intended the latter part of Daly's assertion is open to question, but it served Daly's cause to take it that way, and so be able to reply in a suitably dismissive way:

> I thank Mr Langley for the compliment, but I neither wrote nor orchestrated the 'American'. My only contribution consisted of a few suggestions about reinforcing the score here and there, and I'm not sure that Gershwin, probably with good reason, accepted them. But, then, Gershwin receives many such suggestions from his many friends to whom he always plays his various compositions, light or symphonic, while they are in the process of being written. Possibly Mr Langley feels that we all get together (and we'd have to meet in the Yankee Stadium) and write Mr Gershwin's music for him.

Such a sardonic suggestion rather weakens Daly's position, because Langley's observation was based on first-hand experience, and there is nothing so appropriate for getting to learn about conductors and composers than rehearsing their own works with them. It can become perfectly clear that some conductors depend heavily on having good, reliable professional musicians at their disposal, as indeed composers whose ear is not what it ought to be can have their music revealed to them by performance in this way. Daly went on:

> I would be only too happy to be known as the composer of *An American in Paris*, or of any of the Gershwin works, or as the orchestrator of them. But, alas! I am by trade a conductor (and because Gershwin thinks I am a good one, especially for his music, maybe Mr Langley has been thrown off the scent). It is true that I orchestrate many Gershwin numbers for the theater, but so does Russell Bennett. And I have reduced some of his symphonic works for smaller orchestra for use on the radio. And it is true that we are close friends — to my great profit — and that I use that relationship to criticize. But this is far from the role that Mr Langley suggests.
>
> In fine, the fact is that I have never written one note of any of his compositions, or so much as orchestrated one whole bar of his symphonic works.

That would have been sufficient, since it was a categorical denial, and Daly's letter might have ended there. Instead he chose to weaken that denial by indulging in a certain amount of venom:

> Mr Langley's asseverations are of importance only through the fact that they are now published and are sent abroad in the world to influence those who have no means of checking up on the facts, and to give comfort to those who want to think that Gershwin is a myth.
>
> I suppose I should really resent the fact that Langley attributes Gershwin's work to me, since Langley finds all of it so bad. But fortunately for my *amour-propre*, I have heard some of Langley's compositions. He really should stay away from ink and stick to his viola.

There is a certain amount of begging of questions — who, for example, ever would have had any 'means of checking up on the facts', had they wanted to do so? And how was it that there were definite changes made to the score between its completion and its first performance, as one may see from the manuscript in the Library of Congress? Who suggested the changes, and why? Possibly it was Walter Damrosch, since he would have been in the best position to do so, and presumably Gershwin would have had the confidence in his judgement to accept his suggestions. For the *Concerto* had been improved by similar treatment. In the last analysis, although *An American in Paris* indicates a certain amount of technical progress on Gershwin's part, Olin Downes described it as a 'material gain in workmanship and structure': it's hard to disagree with Downes' further judgement that it 'gets no farther than the earlier works; it reveals no new artistic or emotional ground'. In general, according to Downes, it would be true to say that 'Gershwin sang one song. It is of the city, the music hall'.

The critics were mixed in their reaction to the work, but the audience loved it. The concert had ranked Gershwin alongside César Franck with the Symphony in D minor, Lekeu with the Adagio for Strings and the 'Magic Fire Music' from Wagner's *Die Walküre*. He had at least come out of the experience in one piece. But pieces do not always make a coherent whole, and it is interesting to have the view of someone removed in time from the controversy, and who is yet very similar to Gershwin in many respects — namely, Leonard Bernstein. As he has written: 'When you hear the piece, you rejoice in the first theme, then sit and wait through the 'filler' until the next one comes along. In this way you sit out about two-thirds of the composition. The remaining third is marvelous [US spelling] because it consists of the themes themselves; but where's the composition?'

In the end, however, Bernstein comes down in favour of the piece, and concludes that: 'What's good in it is so good that it's irresistible. If you have to go along with some chaff in order to have the wheat, it's worth it.' Somewhat dangerous ground, perhaps, in the domain of serious music, but then that is to apply the criteria of serious music where they are not necessarily applicable.

It is interesting that Vernon Duke, who heard a good deal of *An American in Paris* when he was in Paris earlier that year with Gershwin, maintained that Gershwin was 1928 in his musical comedies, and in most of his concert music, but that in the concert music 'he allowed himself to become somewhat saccharine in spots' — this according to Ira, who was present on 6 April 1928. One suspects that Duke — who had adopted the name in preference to his original Vladimir Dukelsky at Gershwin's suggestion — was one of the few people who could have been so frank with him, though William Walton is subsequently said to have told Gershwin to ignore Duke's comments. Perhaps, in the context of the period, Walton was right.

In the midst of the celebration of the new work's success, a finger was put on this failure to break, in Olin Downes' words, 'no new artistic or emotional ground'. The occasion was a party given by Jules Glaenzer after the concert, when a brass humidor, engraved with the signatures of several of Gershwin's friends, was to be presented to him by Harry Ruby. However, Ruby had to stay in Boston where a show was causing problems for him, and so his place was taken by the financier Otto H. Kahn, chairman of the board of the Metropolitan Opera. Kahn began his speech by stating quite categorically that 'Gershwin is a leader of young America in music, in the same sense in which Lindbergh is a leader of young America in aviation'. However, he felt that what Gershwin now needed was the experience of some sorrowing or suffering to give him some emotional maturity, or even compassion, one suspects. As Kahn went on:

Now, in that genius of young America, there is one note rather conspicuous by its absence. It is the note that sounds a legacy of sorrow, a note that springs from the deepest stirrings of the soul of the race . . . Now, far be it from me to wish any tragedy to come into the life of this nation for the sake of chastening its soul, or into the life of George Gershwin for the sake of deepening his art. But I do wish to quote him a few verses (by Thomas Hardy, I believe) which I came across the other day and which are supposed to relate to America:

I shrink to see a modern coast
Whose riper times have yet to be;
Where the new regions claim them free
From that long drip of human tears
Which peoples old in tragedy
Have left upon the centuried years.

'The long drip of human tears', my dear George! They have great and strange and beautiful power, those human tears. They fertilize the deepest roots of art, and from them spring flowers of a loveliness and perfume that no other moisture can produce.

95

I believe in you with full faith and admiration — in your personality, your gifts, your art, your future, your significance in the field of American music, and I wish you well with all my heart. And just because of that, I could wish for you an experience, not too prolonged, of that driving storm and stress of the emotions, of that solitary wrestling with your own soul, of that aloofness, for a while, from the actions and distractions of the everyday world, which are the most effective ingredients for the deepening and mellowing and complete development, the energizing and revealment, of an artist's inner being and spiritual powers.

Horace had said very much the same sort of thing, though much more succinctly, centuries ago: *si vis me flere, dolendum est primum ipsi tibi* — 'If you wish to draw tears from me, you must first feel pain yourself.' One cannot claim that suffering is a virtue in itself, but in the absence of it, one feels that it would have taken a far greater composer than Gershwin to fabricate in music the emotions that touch the heart. That is what Kahn was saying to him that evening.

The speech has been read by some — doubtless in view of Kahn's connection with the Metropolitan Opera, one assumes — as a hint that Gershwin ought to write an opera. That seems a rather shallow reading of it, since it is quite clear that Kahn felt that Gershwin still lacked the emotional experience to write such a work. In the event one must assume that Kahn's words went unheeded, and indeed, on the evening on which they were delivered, the general sense of euphoria can hardly have been conducive to taking them very much to heart. Humility was not one of Gershwin's virtues.

6 TO HOLLYWOOD ~ AND BACK

To Hollywood
— and Back

As if to set the seal on the success of 1928, in 1929 Gershwin moved from what had now become the family home on West One Hundred and Third Street to a magnificent penthouse apartment at 33 Riverside Drive, at Seventy-fifth Street. But Ira and his wife had to come, too, since in addition to writing lyrics for his brother, Ira was acting as his business manager, legal adviser and accountant. Ira's legal services were soon to be put to use when the Gershwins collaborated the next year with Florenz Ziegfeld on a new musical, *Show Girl*. The book, by J. P. McEvoy, had been adapted by William Anthony McGuire, and Ira was to work on the lyrics with Gus Kahn, though George alone was to write the music. The show was to open in Boston on 25 June, which may not have been the matter of a couple of weeks' notice that Gershwin himself maintained he had had from Ziegfeld, but nevertheless it was the 'greatest rush job' he had ever had on a score, of that there is no doubt.

Show Girl told of the rise of Dixie Dugan, herself a Ziegfeld girl, from rags to riches, and starred Ruby Keeler, who had married Al Jolson just before the show opened. It was for Ruby Keeler that Gershwin wrote the hit of the show, 'Liza', and on the opening night in Boston, Al Jolson got up from his seat in the auditorium, burst into song, and joined in a chorus of 'Liza' with his wife on stage. It was the sort of occasion that Americans loved — and still do — and delighted the first-night audience. But not all the combined talents of Ruby Keeler, Jimmy Durante, Duke Ellington and a ballet version of *An American in Paris* lasting some fifteen minutes were able to save the show, which ran for only 111 performances. By general consent, *Show Girl* was top heavy with production, and yet Ziegfeld blamed its failure on the Gershwins, to the extent that he refused to pay any royalties due on the songs for the show, and in the end George and Ira were obliged to take him to court. Since Ziegfeld had lost on the Wall Street crash of 1929, one can during his lifetime understand why he wanted to find scapegoats. It was, however, the end of the Gershwins' association with Ziegfeld — though Ira wrote the lyrics for the *Ziegfeld Follies of 1936*, to music by Vernon Duke, after Ziegfeld's death in 1932, and the show was produced by the Shuberts.

According to Gershwin's artist cousin, Henry Botkin, it was in 1929 — the year of the move to the new apartment on Riverside Drive — that the composer started collecting pictures seriously. Botkin was somewhat amazed at the amount of bare space on the walls and set about filling up the spaces with pictures. Botkin's approach, as recalled by himself, was very much in keeping with what Gershwin would probably have done in any case, had the idea occurred to him first. Botkin's suggestion was to visit art galleries, note the works of artists that appealed to them, and when Botkin next went to Paris he would buy some. Botkin also recommended that, in order to appreciate the work of others, Gershwin ought to 'do a little schmeering' on his own. Gershwin took him at his word, and at once acquired canvas and paints. As noted earlier, he had painted his first watercolour two years before that, whilst spending the summer of 1927 in the country, and he had almost always been able to draw in an interesting way.

When Botkin looked back he expressed surprise that he had been able to be so confident in his purchases, since he estimated that he had bought some two hundred or so paintings either for or with Gershwin, and although he had spent seven years in Paris, this by no means provided the whole explanation. In time Gershwin came to acquire works by — amongst others — Modigliani, Derain, Chagall, Rouault and Siqueiros, Utrillo, Kokoschka, Soutine, Gauguin and Tchelitchew. Of Gershwin's own works, the portraits of Jerome Kern, and Arnold Schoenberg even more so, are particularly interesting. There is no doubt that he had a certain amount of talent as an artist, and in some respects one finds correlations between his painting and his music — certainly he said that he wanted to write music in the way that Rouault painted. However, it seems as if his opinion of his talents as an artist matched that of himself as a composer. Bennett Cerf told a story of Gershwin at a dinner-party where he informed the company that a man had told him that he need never write another note of music, since he could make a fortune with his palette and brush. A lady at the table then expressed amazement that one man should possess a genius for two of the arts. Gershwin replied: 'Oh, I don't know. Look at Leonardo da Vinci.'

In the summer of 1929 — on 26 August — Gershwin appeared in a new role, this time as conductor at the Lewisohn Stadium in New York, where he had previously been seen in 1927. He conducted the Philharmonic in a performance of *An American in Paris*, and was the soloist in *Rhapsody in Blue*, which was conducted by Willem van Hoogstraten. Since he had not conducted in public before, Gershwin practised in front of a mirror whilst listening to records of the music with Bill Daly to advise. Edward Kilenyi also claimed that Gershwin came to him for help:

> Before conducting the New York Philharmonic Orchestra in playing his own music at the Lewisohn Stadium one summer — his first experience at conducting a large symphony orchestra — George was worried and asked me what I thought he might do to gain composure. 'Let us go over your music together,' I proposed. He played the records of the music he was about to conduct and which were recorded under his own personal supervision — that is, played the way he wanted them to be played. We spent hours in practice-conducting. I tried to give him all the practical and helpful hints I could give him as a result of my experience in conducting theatre orchestras. His concert was a triumph.

In fact, the recording of *An American in Paris* had not been made entirely 'under his own personal supervision' since Nathaniel Shilkret was the conductor, and became so irritated with Gershwin's constant interference during rehearsals that Shilkret had to ask him to leave until they were finally ready to record. When it came to it, Gershwin played the celesta part in the recording, and managed to miss one of the entries. Nevertheless, the orchestration and general atmosphere of the recording has the genuine feel to it.

It seems that at this time Gershwin was definitely thinking about writing an opera, for he had come across a Jewish play, *The Dybbuk*, the work of S. Ansky, which was the pseudonym of the Polish-Jewish writer Solomon Rappaport (1863–1920). When Gershwin wrote to Isaac Goldberg on 11 October 1928 he said: 'I have been doing a lot of thinking about the *Dybbuk* . . . I have also spoken to Otto Kahn about my idea and he is very eager to have me do the opera. I think something will come of it. I will let you know first hand if anything does. In the meantime do not mention it to anyone.' However, that sort of news was too good for someone to keep to himself or herself, and it was leaked to the press, so that when Gershwin wrote to Goldberg on 23 October, it was to tell him: 'The *Dybbuk* news broke out on the front page of the *Morning Herald* a few days ago and has caused quite a bit of excitement. Other papers writing the news afterward.' The New York *World* even thought it worth the title: 'Gershwin shelves jazz to do opera.'

A week later, on 30 October 1929, Gershwin signed a contract with the Metropolitan Opera for the work to be completed by 1 April 1931. So certain did it all seem, that the opera was projected for either the season of 1931–2 or 1932–3, with exclusive performances for the company in New York, Brooklyn, Philadelphia, Baltimore, Washington, Atlanta and Cleveland. Gershwin made some sketches for the work, which do not seem to have survived, unfortunately, and even considered going to Europe to study Jewish music. However, the whole project floundered when it was discovered that the rights to the play had been assigned already to the Italian composer Lodovico Rocca, and his work had its première at La Scala, Milan, in 1934.

If Gershwin felt thwarted in his aim to become an operatic composer at this time, after the Lewisohn Stadium success, he had decided that he had added conducting to his list of talents, and accepted an invitation to repeat his interpretation of *An American in Paris* in November, this time with the newly formed Manhattan Symphony Orchestra, whose director was the composer and conductor Henry Hadley (1871–1937), at the Mecca Temple (now the City Center) on West Fifty-fifth Street. And it was on the crest of the same wave that Gershwin decided that he would direct the orchestra in the pit for the opening of his next show, the revived *Strike Up the Band*, which opened on Christmas Eve, 1929, at the Shubert Theater in Boston, and then on 14 January 1930 at the Times Square Theater on Broadway, though Hilding Anderson was the regular conductor.

After its disastrous debut in August 1927, Morrie Ryskind had been drafted in to tone down the book in an attempt to make it more palatable to the public, since it was felt that the anti-war stance had been one of the biggest factors in its failure. This time it was well received, though it only lasted for 191 performances, which by now were not many for a Gershwin musical, but one must remember that it followed the Wall Street Crash of 29 October 1929, and in the circumstances, therefore, did not do too badly at all. Moreover, the complete vocal score was published, and this was only the second Gershwin show to be given such an accolade.

The seemingly indefatigable Vernon Duke took the equally indefatigable Prokofiev to the opening night in New York, and then to a party afterwards at the Warburg home. As Duke put it, 'there was no room for nostalgia but . . . the music was better'. In Duke's account Gershwin played the piano until the notices arrived, and since they were all excellent, he 'resumed his recital with renewed vigour'. When asked by Russel Crouse how he liked the show, Gershwin's father replied: 'What do you mean how do I like it? I *have* to like it.'

The second show of 1930 was *Girl Crazy*, an Aarons–Freedley production that was to open at the Alvin Theater on 14 October. The book, by Guy Bolton and John McGowan, is a satire on the Far West, and tells how handsome, wealthy New Yorker, Danny Churchill (played by Allen Kearns) is sent by his worried father to remote Custerville in Arizona in order to keep him out of tempta- tion's way. Danny makes the journey from New York to Custerville in a taxi, driven by Gieber Goldfarb (played by Willie Howard), who subsequently becomes sheriff of the town. Danny sets up a fake ranch, where he simply continues his wicked ways by importing a batch of chorus girls. In the end, of course, Danny falls for Mollie Gray, the demure postmistress of the town, played by Ginger Rogers, recently seen in the Broadway show *Top Speed* and the film *Young Man of Manhattan*. A newcomer to Broadway was Ethel Merman, who played Frisco Kate, a bar-room tough girl with a soft interior. Each word she uttered could be heard in every part of the theatre, and when she delivered 'I Got Rhythm' she stopped the show.

When Vinton Freedley took her to the Riverside Drive apart- ment for an audition, Ethel Merman had never met Gershwin before, so that in prospect for her it 'was like meeting God'. Not even in her wildest dreams had she ever imagined that 'the great Gershwin' would be sitting down at the keyboard to play his songs for her. She was completely taken aback, however, when, after playing 'I Got Rhythm', he told her that if there was anything about the song she didn't like, he would be happy to change it for her. Miss Merman was tongue-tied — for once — and simply nodded and smiled. Like the good trouper she was, she was busy trying to think how to phrase the music, she later maintained, but for Gershwin, who needed the immediate response, and preferably a favourable one, the lack of reaction was worrying. Again he offered to make changes if there was anything in the song that Miss Merman took exception to. As she herself put it: 'It wasn't that; it was only that I was so flabbergasted. Through the fog that had wrapped itself around me, I heard myself say, "They'll do very nicely, Mr Gershwin".'

When Ethel Merman told friends of this meeting subsequently, they felt that it gave the impression that she had given Gershwin the 'old hauteur treatment', but as she observed, at that point in her career: 'I was so drunk with the glory of it all that I could have said anything, but whatever I said, I meant it to be grateful and humble. That's for sure.' When she and Gershwin met for lunch the day after the New York opening, he asked her if she had seen the reviews. It was typical that he should have seen them all, but she had been so late to bed the night before that she had only risen in time for her luncheon. When she indicated that she had not, he told her: 'They're raves, all of them. You're in with both feet.'

Ethel Merman was not the only good thing about *Girl Crazy*, nor the only member of the company to make an impression, and there were other good tunes such as 'Embraceable You' and 'But Not for Me', which subsequently became staunch Gershwin favourites. For a show playing during the Depression, its 272 performances were fairly remarkable, but perhaps even more remarkable for posterity was the personnel of the orchestra, Red Nichols and his band, which included Jimmy Dorsey, Benny Goodman, Gene Krupa, Glen Miller and Jack Teagarden. Not surprisingly, in view of his new-found confidence, Gershwin decided to take up the baton again for the première. On 16 October, two days after the opening night, he wrote to Isaac Goldberg, who was already working on Gershwin's biography by this time:

I am just recuperating from a couple of exciting days. I worked very hard conducting the orchestra and dress rehearsal and finally the opening night, when the theater was so warm that I must have lost at least three pounds, perspiring. The opening was so well received that five pounds would not have been too much. With the exception of some dead head friends of mine, who sat in the front row, everybody seemed to enjoy the show tremendously, especially the critics. I think the notices, especially of the music, were the best I have ever received. Did you see them, by any chance? The show looks so good that I can leave in a few weeks for Hollywood, with the warm feeling that I have a hit under the belt. When are you coming down to see the show and me?

That single reference to Hollywood indicated the next direction that this seemingly charmed career was to take, though the plans had been laid as early as April of that year (1930), when George and Ira had signed a contract with Fox Studios for a musical film entitled *Delicious*, with Janet Gaynor and Charles Farrell. It was not until November, however, that the Gershwins eventually left for the West Coast.

There was a certain amount of resistance to Hollywood in some of the more diehard New York theatre circles — despite the fact that several Broadway composers had been lured out there — so that the decision of the Gershwins to accept was applauded by the cinema editor of the New York *American*: 'The Gershwins both are staunch in their loyalty to the screen and its potentialities. Each refuse[s] to take Hollywood with the tongue-in-cheek sneering that has come to be considered the smart attitude along Broadway.'

Gershwin's dealings with the world of motion pictures had begun as early as 1923, when he and Ira, still then using the pseudonym Arthur Francis, had provided a score for a silent film, *The Sunshine Trail*. But it was not until 1930 that there was further involvement, when the Fox Studios contract was signed in April and when a film about Paul Whiteman entitled *The King of Jazz* opened at the Roxy in New York the next month. For two weeks Gershwin appeared live as the soloist in *Rhapsody in Blue*, with Paul Whiteman, on the stage of what he called 'Roxy's Cathedral'. For granting permission for the use of his music in this film, Gershwin collected $50,000. Under the terms of the Fox Studios contract for *Delicious*, George was to be paid $70,000 and Ira $30,000, which was generous by any standards, but particularly in the Depression. But then Hollywood was riding the crest of a great wave with sound-film production still relatively new (since 1926), though musicals themselves were temporarily on the wane by 1930, because they had lost the impact they had had when they were brand new.

Before Gershwin left for the West Coast, however, there were various undertakings, including a return to the Lewisohn Stadium on 28 August (1930) for his third appearance there. On this occasion he conducted *An American in Paris* and was soloist in both *Rhapsody in Blue* and *Concerto in F* with Willem van Hoogstraten conducting. The crowd this time seems to have been rather less than before — possibly only some 13,000 people — though still large by any standards when compared with the usual audience for an orchestral concert.

Then there was a great flurry of family activity at the beginning of November, just before Gershwin was about to take the train for Hollywood, and his parents were due to leave before him to winter in Florida. Frances Gershwin was in love with Leopold Godowsky, Jr., but her mother did not want her daughter to marry him or even see him. On his return from a trip to Europe on 1 November, Leo realized that, with the Gershwin parents in Florida and George and Ira in Hollywood, the chances of a wedding with the family's blessing were highly remote, and yet at the same time he did not want to do anything behind their backs, in their absence. The first of November was a Saturday, and the Gershwin parents were due to leave the next day for Florida, on the six o'clock train. Leo was not to be deterred. He called a friend, Judge Botein, in the early hours of Sunday morning, and discovered from him that there was a place in the Bronx where he could obtain a marriage licence, and he also arranged for a jeweller to meet Frances that afternoon to choose a wedding ring. They still needed someone to perform the ceremony, however, so Leo decided to look in the telephone book for the names of the 'reverends' in the neighbourhood who might conceivably be Jewish. By the time they found someone it was four p.m., but the rabbi agreed to come because he was a music lover and recognized the name of Gershwin.

Then came the terrifying business of telling Mrs Gershwin. As Frances herself put it: 'I was scared to tell my mother because she blamed her asthma a great deal on the fact that I was going with Leo. Anyway, we went up to the apartment and told her, and there was really nothing she could do about it, as it was all arranged.'

What followed was rather like a stage farce. George came in from his adjoining penthouse to Ira's where everyone else was assembled, but despite the occasion, and the time of day, he was dressed in pyjamas and dressing-gown and smoking a large cigar. The rabbi then appeared from the same direction, having gone to George's apartment first. Mr Gershwin senior kept looking at his watch and telling his wife that they ought to leave if they were to catch their train. The bride had no flowers, but Kay Swift had sent some to Mrs Gershwin as a parting present, so they did service for Frances instead. George obliged with the wedding march at the piano — a shortened version of *Rhapsody in Blue* — and the rabbi started talking about rhythm and harmony, using all the technical terms he could muster up in such company. As soon as the ceremony was over, the company rushed off to the railway station, not to see off the bridal couple, but Mr and Mrs Gershwin on their holiday.

That evening Bert Taylor, Gertrude Lawrence's current boy-friend, held a farewell party for George and Ira that almost turned into a wedding reception for Frances and Leo, since George went around telling everyone about the very recent marriage.

Soon, then, it was the turn of George and Ira to leave, which they did on the following Wednesday, 5 November. Also on the train were Guy Bolton, Nicholas Schenck and Edgar Selwyn (who were brothers-in-law), and several other members of the party.

In a way it was virtually inevitable that Gershwin should have gone to Hollywood, since he was such a leading light in his generation, and the cinema attracted talent like a great magnet because it, too, was the leading medium of entertainment. And Gershwin himself professed — at least in public — to be going to this new world with appropriate humility: 'I go to work for the talkies like any other amateur, for I know very little about them. Because I am inexperienced with films, I am approaching them in a humble state of mind.' Or so he told Isaac Goldberg, who published those words in the Boston *Evening Transcript* on 29 November. It is hard to believe that Gershwin ever regarded himself 'like any other amateur', however, no matter what he undertook.

George, Ira and Lee shared a house together, 1027 Chevy Chase, Beverly Hills, which had previously been inhabited by Greta Garbo. George even slept in the bed that she had used, though he had to admit that it had not helped him to sleep any better. He worked mainly at home with Ira, but there was a cottage reserved for them at the Fox Studios, to which they could retreat if necessary. Before the end of the year Gershwin had written much of the music for the film, though in fact many of the songs were adaptations of existing material. There was, however, to be music to accompany a dream sequence in the film, and a depiction of

Manhattan in a rhapsody or fantasy which in time was expanded
into the *Second Rhapsody*. In the event, only about a minute of the
rhapsody music was used in the film, of some six that Gershwin
wrote for it.

Life was not all work, however, in Hollywood — as the *Herald
Tribune* quoted Gershwin on 3 March 1931, after his return: 'I
worked hard in Hollywood, but did manage to bring my golf score
down a few points.' And there were concerts, too, like the one given
on 15 January (1931), when Arthur Rodzinski conducted the Los
Angeles Philharmonic in *An American in Paris*.

What Gershwin had not realized, however, was that once he had
written the music for *Delicious* and handed it over, then his
connection with the film ceased. Despite the fact that he told New
York friends that he would have to go back to California in July
1931 for three weeks to supervise the making of the film, there was
really no need for him to do so, since he had recorded all the songs
before he left, so that the studio would be in no doubt about the
tempi. A singer from one of Paul Whiteman's bands was engaged
for $50 to croon the lyrics, and so it was that someone called Bing
Crosby made one of his early appearances in the annals of music
history.

When *Delicious* was released in December 1931, some of the songs
had been omitted, and only a portion of the rhapsody used. The
critic of *Outlook and Independent* declared: 'George Gershwin is said to
have written the music involved, but you'd never know it . . .
Civilization hasn't had such a setback since the Dark Ages.'
Despite this disappointment, at least it meant that when the
Gershwins had left Hollywood on 22 February 1931 to return to
New York they had taken with them not only the first draft of the
Second Rhapsody, but some of the songs for a new musical, *Of Thee I
Sing*.

The *Rhapsody* went through several metamorphoses of title before
it ended up in its more serious guise. It had been *Manhattan
Rhapsody*, then *New York Rhapsody* in the final script of the film, and
Gershwin even thought of it as *Rhapsody in Rivets* at one point, since
he had found a melody that evoked riveting to depict the bustle of
Manhattan. As he wrote to Isaac Goldberg in a letter of 30 June
1931: 'As part of the picture where it is to be played takes place in
many streets of New York, I used as a starting-point what I called
"a rivet theme" but, after that, I just wrote a piece of music without
a program.' In the same letter he went on to analyse his motives in

writing the *Rhapsody*: 'I wrote it mainly because I wanted to write a serious composition and found the opportunity in California. Nearly everybody comes back from California with a western tan and a pocketful of motion-picture money. I decided to come back with both these things and a serious composition — if the climate would let me. I was under no obligation to the Fox Company to write this. But, you know, the old artistic soul must be appeased every so often.'

Gershwin had begun orchestrating the *Rhapsody* on 14 March and completed it on 23 May 1931, according to his own annotation on the manuscript. The title was now *Second Rhapsody for Orchestra with Piano*, and the point of this, as Gershwin himself, in the letter to Goldberg referred to above, explained, was that: 'Although the piano has quite a few solo parts, I may make it just one of the orchestral instruments, instead of solo.' A few days before he wrote to Goldberg, on 26 June, he had engaged an orchestra to play through the work with him as pianist, in the studios of the National Broadcasting Company, and Victor had made a private recording for him. He felt confident enough to tell Goldberg: 'In many respects, such as orchestration and form, it is the best thing I've written.'

Gershwin decided to dedicate the work to Max Dreyfus, as a token of gratitude for all that the publisher had done for him. Dreyfus was in London when he heard about the dedication, and it was from there that he cabled Gershwin, telling him that he was 'touched beyond words'. He also said that it was about the nicest thing that had happened to him.

The work was destined not to have its first public performance until January of the following year (1932), and at least part of the reason for this was that some time after his return from Hollywood, Gershwin had met Arturo Toscanini at the home of the critic Samuel Chotzinoff. Gershwin played piano versions of both *Rhapsody in Blue* and the *Second Rhapsody* to the great conductor on that occasion, and — perhaps somewhat to Gershwin's surprise — Toscanini seemed not to know his compositions. Nevertheless, Toscanini gave the impression of liking the music to the extent that Gershwin had hopes that he might give the first performance of the new work with the New York Philharmonic — though it must be stressed that Toscanini gave no sort of commitment on this occasion. Then William Paley, head of CBS, was also treated to a piano rendition from Gershwin at a party, and implied that he would see what he could do to persuade Toscanini to give the work its first performance. In the event, however, it was Serge Koussevitzky and the Boston Symphony who gave the first performance, in Boston, on 29 January 1932, and then in New York on 5 February that year.

In fact, Gershwin had been playing fast and loose with Koussevitzky, for as long ago as 28 October 1929 the conductor had written to him — in response to overtures from Vernon Duke ('Mr Dukelsky') on Gershwin's behalf — indicating that he was aware that Gershwin would like him to perform some of his works, and in a generous gesture Koussevitzky not only promised to do so, but also requested that Gershwin should write something for the Boston Symphony Orchestra, since the following season was to be their fiftieth anniversary. In this way Koussevitzky commissioned several works from Gershwin.

Koussevitzky was a generous patron of young composers, and spent a great deal of his life commissioning and conducting contemporary music. He was born near Tver in Russia in 1874, became a virtuoso double-bass player, and spent a period of time in Paris before eventually going to America, where he conducted the Boston Symphony Orchestra from 1924 until 1949. In Russia he had encouraged Scriabin, Stravinsky and Prokofiev, and in Paris, Ravel and Honegger. Now, in a third wave of activity, he met a young composer of Russian extraction in Gershwin who was decidedly American. But it was not simply a matter of home from home: Koussevitzky had a genuine and positive doctrine about composers and their works:

> Every great, or less great, or even little, composer brings something to the art of music which makes the art great in its entirety. Each one brings his portion. In examination of his music we can see how real a composer is. We can see whether his technique is perfect; whether he knows how the orchestra and the individual instruments sound and whether or not he has something to say, no matter what the degree of importance. Sometimes a single man has one single word to say all his life and that one word may be as important as the life work of a great genius. We need that word — and so does the genius himself need that word.

This rather Russian way of seeing all things as part of some great entity informed Koussevitzky's whole approach to music, and enabled him to put Gershwin alongside Stravinsky, for which the former ought to have been extremely grateful, rather than look to the more obviously famous Toscanini, who was not interested in any case.

If Gershwin was disappointed that Toscanini had not seen fit to play his work, he ought to have taken consolation from the fact that when Toscanini did eventually conduct some Gershwin, a performance of *Rhapsody in Blue* on 1 November 1942, Virgil Thomson wrote in the *Herald Tribune*: 'It all came off like a ton of bricks . . . It was as far from George's own way of playing the piece as one could imagine.' Earl Wild had been the soloist on that occasion. Koussevitzky, on the other hand, served Gershwin well, and of course the composer was the soloist on both occasions. As Isaac Goldberg reported in the Boston *Evening Transcript* the day after the première, Gershwin said of the conductor: 'The man is marvelous. He knows the score inside out.' And of the Boston Symphony: 'What sight-readers his players are! It's great to feel that you're in such wonderful hands.' To some extent the feeling was mutual between Gershwin and Koussevitzky, for in the year after Gershwin's death, the conductor said of him that he was an 'extraordinary being too great to be real'.

The day after the first New York performance, Lawrence Gilman, writing in the *Herald Tribune*, likened Gershwin to Paderewski — at least by inference — but Gershwin's piano technique was simply nowhere near that class. Oscar Levant, in his book *A Smattering of Ignorance*, told how he competed with Gershwin, shortly before the period in question, for the favours of a girl from the chorus of *Strike Up the Band* (1930 version). Levant observed that Gershwin's fur-trimmed overcoat, of positively ducal appearance, which made him look like a 'perpetual guest conductor', gave him the edge over himself as far as the girl was concerned. However, she was also a devotee of *La Bohème*, and as Levant observed: 'George had difficulty in playing the Puccini score for her on the piano for two reasons: (A) It wasn't by Gershwin. (B) He didn't read other people's music very well (at that time).' Despite Levant's parenthetical implication that Gershwin's sight-reading improved, there is little genuine evidence that it ever did, and in any case the over-riding fact remains that he simply did not play other people's compositions, or certainly not in public.

Leaving aside his playing, the reaction of the critics was that the

Second Rhapsody had not lived up to either the *Rhapsody in Blue* or Gershwin's own claims for his new piece. Although, as mentioned above, he had begun with a reference to Paderewski, Lawrence Gilman was by no means so kind when it came to the music itself. In fact, he turned Gershwin's words against himself. In an unfortunate flight of fancy, Gershwin had said that in finding the second theme for his new rhapsody, he had 'wanted merely to write a broad, flowing melody, the same as Bach, Brahms or Wagner would have done'. As Gilman observed: 'Needless to say, he gives us, also, music employing those idioms with which, long since, he caught the ear of the world.' Well, that may not have been in itself a bad thing, but unfortunately one feels that by this time Gershwin really had put himself in the same league as Bach, Brahms and Wagner — at least in his own imagination.

Olin Downes, writing in the *Times*, paid tribute to Koussevitzky's conducting and Gershwin's playing of what he described as a 'modest' piano part, but criticised adversely the fact that Gershwin had copied himself, since the *Second Rhapsody* was 'imitative in many ways of the *Rhapsody in Blue*', which he found 'more individual and originative' than the new *Rhapsody*, which was, in any case, 'too long for its material'. It was said that when Gershwin was trying to decide what to call the rhapsody, his father suggested — apparently in all seriousness — *Rhapsody in Blue No. 2*. In that way, he went on, his son could write *Rhapsody in Blue No. 3, No. 4* and *No. 5* — 'you know, just like Beethoven.'

Despite Gershwin's somewhat pretentious remark to Isaac Goldberg about 'the old artistic soul' being appeased every so often — as if it were some physical need that required satisfaction and then, presumably, to be consigned to oblivion, instead of leading to the genesis of some new creation — it is hard to believe that the *Second Rhapsody* was anything more than a piece of cool calculation on Gershwin's part which turned out to be a miscalculation of the first order. Toscanini may even have been more perspicacious than Gershwin gave him credit for when treated to his private performance of the work, but it is unlikely that Gershwin would have been aware of that. And it is easy, yet again, to damn Gershwin with his own words. He was reported as saying, apropos Arthur Honegger: 'The European boys have small ideas but they sure know how to dress 'em up.' The sad truth of the matter is that if the *Second Rhapsody* had had even 'small ideas', and Gershwin the expertise of Honegger, the piece might have been redeemed, but there is nothing at the heart of it. There are no tunes, which is all the more sad that Gershwin thought it so good:

> I had seven weeks in California. The amount of music which the picture required was small and quickly written. The parties and night life of Hollywood did not interest me in the least. They bored me in fact. Here was my chance to do some serious work. Seven weeks of almost uninterrupted opportunity to write the best music I could possibly think of! What a chance.

Even there, it seems that Gershwin was trying to fool himself — or at least the readership — since from Ira's letter from Hollywood to the Paleys, written the day after the Los Angeles performance of *An American in Paris* on 15 January 1931, there had been an endless succession of dinner-parties, and George was often invited for week-ends and on trips here and there, including down to Mexico. But, in the end, if the music speaks to people and provides them with something they might otherwise not have heard or enjoyed, then one must accept the fact, and it is consistent with what Koussevitzky proclaimed. Time will have to have the last word on the *Second Rhapsody*.

7 OF THEE I SING

Of Thee I Sing

Gershwin came through the Depression years financially unscathed, and indeed there is precious little reference to it at all in records of his conversations with others or in letters he wrote during that period. Doubtless he had known a certain amount of poverty in his childhood, no matter what his mother maintained about their situation at any one time, and he had the determination to be successful and stay at the top of the tree for as long as he could. He was in any case so busy that although he knew what had happened, since it had touched colleagues, too, he simply kept on working. And in some respects, by continuing to write music and give the public entertainment, he was doing something to alleviate the gloom.

Nevertheless, there is little or no evidence that he saw his role in that light, and it seems yet another aspect of his personality in which compassion seems to have been absent for much of the time. Charity does not seem to have been very high on his list of priorities. It is true that he gave money for musical scholarships when Schoenberg came to America, though that is one of the few recorded instances. Another was when he played in a concert for unemployed musicians at the Metropolitan Opera House. And of course he made sure that his family never went without, and that, too, was right and proper. But this lack of compassion affected his mental attitude to others, even those who might well have been thought of as close friends and colleagues, and also any potential wife.

Time and time again, as he grew older, Gershwin sensed the need for a wife, and talked about that need to others, but somehow he never seemed to make a permanent bond. To some extent his career and the sheer amount of work it involved, was a valid excuse, but he was so much in the company of some of the most beautiful women of his day that he had no problem whatsoever in meeting them. It was rather that the lack of will to form an attachment, and his concern with himself, his career and his health, were all serious impediments to finding a partner in life. Indeed, from the evidence that others provided, some women virtually threw themselves, so to speak, at his feet, and he may well have taken advantage of the fact on occasion, but there's little firm evidence of this, and, if he did, then it would seem that he never bothered to see if any of them could have provided him with lasting companionship and happiness. But there were, however, one or two exceptions.

It is from the summer of 1931 that we have some of the few love letters from Gershwin that have been made public, written to Rosamond Walling Tirana, twelve years his junior. Rosamond was distantly related to Gershwin by marriage, since she was a cousin of Emily Strunsky Paley, whose sister, Leonore, was Ira Gershwin's wife. In fact, George and Rosamond first met at Emily's wedding, when she was seven and he was eighteen. Later she became the intelligent college girl from Swarthmore, Pennsylvania, and he the famous composer who had left school at the age of fifteen and made his own way in life. As before, in Gershwin's emotional attachments, there was a considerable element of attraction of opposites. She knew nothing about music.

Rosamond especially remembered the occasion in 1928 when she went with the Strunskys to greet the Gershwins on their return from Europe. They all went back to 103rd Street, and George singled her out to give her two presents: a black and white cigarette case with cubist inlay, and a gold bracelet set with emeralds, rubies and little pearls. He had found the latter in an antique shop in Paris, and told her that it reminded him of her — saying that it looked as if it had a Russian soul. Anything more calculated to devastate such a young, impressionable girl would be hard to imagine. The very knowledge that he had even thought of her whilst he was abroad must have been sufficient in itself to sweep her off her feet.

Whenever she could get away from Swarthmore, Rosamond would join Gershwin in New York, Atlantic City or Philadelphia, but she stayed with Leonore and Ira, since Gershwin was always fastidious in his behaviour towards her. In later years, however, she freely confessed that his ideas about marriage held no charm for her. He wanted four children as a start, with a country estate and horses for them. She, on the other hand, hoped never to see Westchester County again, and did not want children for at least ten years. Despite Gershwin's flattering attentions, some of his comments to her, as she recorded herself, can hardly have endeared him to women: he told her that she could be good for his stomach, that his friends liked her, that if she could learn to keep her stockings straight and get her run-down heels changed she might be glamorous, except that her dress was terrible, and the skirt far too short for current fashion. He made a deal that if she helped him to buy some paints, he would get her something that would cover her knees. At one stage she was even going to move into the apartment building on Riverside Drive, to the downstairs apartment, from which they would construct an interior staircase so that she could have privacy and paint. The reason she gave for not moving in eventually was that she did not like the decoration when it was complete. However, it is far from clear that matrimony was intended at that time, although Gershwin had often referred to it.

During the summer of 1931, Rosamond Walling was in London, and the letters were written to her then. One, dated 5 September, is most revealing:

> You certainly have made an indelible impression on my friends. Only last night Billy Seeman said you were the nicest girl he had ever seen me with. Often when I think of you I get a desire to fly over to where you are, swoop down like an eagle and steal you and bring you to a big rock on a mountain and there have you all to myself. And I may do it someday.

But he never did. And as Rosamond Walling knew, despite his 'heavenly eyes', he did not need her, and he never made her feel needed. After all, he had reached fame and fortune without her, and he seemed all set to go on to even greater achievement. But he mocked her because she seemed to want the romantic love that might be offered by a poor artist or writer or scholar, rather than the success and security that he could offer. Tragically, that was all he had to offer, it would seem, for here was a person prepared to dedicate her life to him, and he did not seem to want that, let alone be prepared to dedicate his life to her — or to anyone else, for that matter.

It seems a curious contradiction, to say the least, that for one who devoted so much time to love in his songs, Gershwin seems to have been so far removed from knowing what it really was. It has been said that the lyrics of 'Where's The Boy', which Ira wrote for *Treasure Girl*, contain the quintessence of the plot of every musical of the Twenties:

There is no doubt
    About
The fact that life without
    A lord and master
Is a disaster.

There is a 'he'
    Who'd be
The world and all to me
    But fate decided
    We be divided.

There's just this man and it's high time
He came to take up my time.
    Will he appear?
        Oh dear!
Each day seems like a year
But who knows whether
We'll get together.

And in a way Gershwin knew this full well. During the run of *Of Thee I Sing*, at one performance Gershwin was standing at the back of the Music Box Theater with George Kaufman, who wrote the book with Ryskind, and as the audience delighted in their combined efforts, Kaufman said to Gershwin: 'What's the matter with them? Don't they know we're kidding love?' Gershwin did not agree, however: 'You may think you're kidding love, but when John P. Wintergreen faces impeachment to stand by the girl he married, that's championing love — and the audience knows it.' Ira, too, knew what love meant to the Gershwins, though in a rather different way. 'Don't knock love, my boy. Without it, I'd be out of business.' George's tragedy was that he really needed the sort of love he so often wrote songs about, but for one reason or another — and the letters to Rosamond Walling give some of them — he was unable to form the vital bond.

120

In the letters to Rosamond, Gershwin referred to some of his activities of that summer of 1931, such as the play-through of the new rhapsody; the fact that Frances and Leo were to go and live in Rochester for two years; the short-wave broadcast to Germany of the second movement of the *Concerto*, under Damrosch, in August, as well as another concert at the Lewisohn Stadium, when Bill Daly made his debut as a symphony conductor. Gershwin also gave up smoking that summer, played at the opening of the Manhattan Theater on 5 August, and was invited to tour Europe as soloist with Albert Coates conducting — but he was also working on the new show for Aarons and Freedley, *Of Thee I Sing*.

As early as November 1930, when the Gershwin brothers had left for Hollywood, they had taken with them an outline, which ran to fourteen pages, for the book of *Of Thee I Sing*, by George S. Kaufman and Morrie Ryskind. They had come back with two of the tunes virtually already written. As before, Gershwin used material originally conceived for other shows — though in fact only two numbers in this case — and the show was ready for December 1931.

The story deals with the business of American politics in a highly satirical way. The political barons decide on a presidential candidate — John P. (for Peppermint) Wintergreen — and then proceed with the election campaign. One of the gimmicks is a beauty contest in Atlantic City, when the prize offered to the winner is marriage with the candidate, so that she becomes the first lady when he is elected. Things begin to go wrong, however, when Wintergreen falls in love with his secretary, Mary Turner, instead of the eventual winner of the beauty contest, Diana Devereaux. Wintergreen refuses to relent, however, and rallies the voters to him with the slogan: 'Lovers! Vote for John and Mary!' As the song puts it, 'Love is Sweeping the Country' on election day, and Wintergreen is swept into office on its tide. There is a double ceremony when Wintergreen is inaugurated as president and is married to Mary Turner at the same time, before the Supreme Court and Congress.

However, all is not destined to remain sweetness and light for long. The French government protests, through its ambassador in Washington, that Wintergreen ought to have married Diana Devereaux as originally promised, and that in not doing so, the new president has mortally offended French national pride. Diana Devereaux, it would seem, is the illegitimate daughter of an

121

illegitimate son of an illegitimate nephew of Napoleon Bonaparte. (The song 'The Illegitimate Daughter' had been completed first, in Hollywood.) Pressure now grows from both Washington and France for Wintergreen to divorce Mary and marry Diana Devereaux, but he refuses to do so, and the Senate has to decide whether he is to be impeached or not. Mary saves the day with the dramatic announcement that she is to become a mother. In the event, she gives birth to twins.

If the idea sounds rather jejune, and today somewhat self-conscious when heard on the stage, nevertheless the show was historically important. George Jean Nathan called it a 'landmark in American satirical comedy', and Brooks Atkinson in the *New York Times* described it as 'a taut and lethal satire on national politics'. He said that the show was 'funnier than the government, and not nearly so dangerous'. Taut was an apt epithet, since there is a tautness in the show, in the integration of the various elements — not least that between score and book — that was rare for its time, and rare in Gershwin's work. It became the first musical to win the Pulitzer Prize (2 May 1932), and one may appreciate why it did. As Gershwin himself said:

> It was one of those rare shows in which everything clicked just right. After the opening there was little or no 'fixing' to do . . . One show that I'm more proud of than any I have written. I don't suppose it's hard to guess which one it is and there's no suspense about it. I might as well tell you the name — it is *Of Thee I Sing*. This is the only musical comedy ever to be awarded a Pulitzer Prize. You remember what my father said when the prize was given. He said, 'That Pulitzer must be a smart man.'

Morris Gershwin died less than two weeks later, on 15 May 1932.

There is a total lack of information as to how Gershwin felt about his father's death. Reading between the lines of Frances Gershwin's recollections, however, one is tempted to feel that, despite the outward show of affection, there was considerable unease amongst the children at Morris's personality and character. He never lost his Russian-Jewish accent, and when George went to parties he would tell stories about his father, and imitate his accent. In Frances' estimation this showed that George had no false pride about such things. She admitted, however, that certainly as a young girl she was ashamed of her father's accent, especially when she had to introduce him to her friends. Later, from her confident position in society, she could say that her father was 'a darling person', a 'real shnook', but all the same, one suspects that Morris Gershwin was something of an ordeal for his children, and it was only when George reached fame and fortune that he felt he could carry off the paternal existence as some kind of affable eccentricity, and not make fun of it, or excuses for it. Did Morris's demise, then, come as something of a relief? Of course it could not be admitted, but it was certainly true that Gershwin and his mother became closer to each other after it. If nothing else, it was pleasant to think that Morris had seen his daughter and two of his sons financially established, and the work of the last two acknowledged with the award of the Pulitzer, before he died. Because of the rules then in operation, however, only the authors and lyricists actually received the prize, the composer could not be recognized.

Pulitzer Prize apart, *Of Thee I Sing* ran for 441 performances. It had a try-out in Boston, at the Majestic Theater, opening on 8 December 1931, and then at the Music Box Theater on Broadway on 26 December.

Despite Gershwin's account of the ease of its preparation and production, all had not been quite so relaxed. Gershwin brought many friends to the rehearsals, which irritated Kaufman, who disliked being watched when he was directing. After one rehearsal he was moved to say to Gershwin: 'This show is going to be a terrible flop. The balcony was only half filled today.' Kaufman's acid wit was also applied to William Gaxton, who played Wintergreen in the show. He took so many liberties with the script that Kaufman was finally impelled to send him a telegram: 'I am watching your performance from the rear of the house. Wish you were here.' Kaufman's faith in the book was not misplaced. When representatives of the Franco-American Society complained to him about the way in which the French Ambassador was treated in the show, and the references to France's unpaid war debts to America, Kaufman replied that he was willing to make changes if they could come up with situations or lines for the show that were funnier than the originals. He had identified his targets well. Particularly accurate is the way in which the role of Vice-President is handled in the show. Alexander Throttlebottom, played by Victor Moore, was so little-known in Washington when he became Vice-President that he had to join a guided tour to get into the White House.

However, the show has not done well in revivals, and when it was brought back to New York in 1969, Clive Barnes was moved to write in the *New York Times* on 8 March: 'It is not just bad, it is terrible.' And he went on to add: 'Nor is this entirely a matter of changing tastes, except in the respect that we do demand a new standard of wit and even literacy from our musical books nowadays.' But as far as the score was concerned, he was much more favourably inclined:

> This is an extraordinarily advanced kind of musical comedy. The Gershwins were here actually straining towards proper, or more likely improper, operetta, and had the courage to use arias, ensembles, even, as unlikely as it sounds, recitatives, and the musical aspect of the show is as new as tomorrow. They don't write musical scores like that anymore, but let's live in hope.

When the show was revived in 1972 for television, the *New York Times* reviewer (on this occasion John J. O'Connor) again praised the music, but of the show itself wrote: 'Back in 1931, *Of Thee I Sing* hit the Broadway musical stage and thousands cheered. Millions may wonder what the cheering was all about.'

December 1931 had certainly been Gershwin's month, with the film *Delicious* released on the 3rd of that month, *Of Thee I Sing* opening in Boston on the 8th and then in New York on the 26th, and Gershwin was able to write to a friend on 2 January 1932: 'The New Year is here. *Of Thee I Sing* is the town's big hit, having gotten the most sensational reviews of many a day from the New York critics.' And he was able to add: 'The picture, *Delicious*, has just turned in the best week's receipts in three years.' At the end of January 1932 came the Boston première of *Second Rhapsody*, and the New York première on 5 February. So Gershwin went on into 1932, and it was just as busy a year as the previous one had been. He had been planning another trip to Europe, but his father's death, among other things, prevented that. However, he had managed to fit in a visit to Havana, in February, which inspired the orchestral piece *Rumba*, better known as *Cuban Overture*.

Gershwin began the composition of the *Rumba* — as it is named on the title-page of his score — in July 1932 and was able to begin the orchestration on 1 August, finishing it on the 9th, ready for an all-Gershwin concert at the Lewisohn Stadium on 16 August. He had been impressed with the percussion sounds he had heard in Cuba, and brought back with him claves (or Cuban hardwood sticks), bongos, guiro (a serrated gourd rubbed with a wooden stick), and maracas. There is a note on the title-page of the score for the conductor, that the Cuban instruments should be right in front of the conductor's stand, and so that there should be no doubt as to what was intended, each instrument is drawn and labelled, and the conductor's place at the podium is drawn at the bottom of the page.

Gershwin provided his own commentary for the work by way of a programme note, which conspicuously lacks the more spontaneous Gershwin touch:

> In my composition I have endeavored to combine the Cuban rhythms with my own thematic material. The result is a symphonic overture which embodies the essence of the Cuban dance. It has three main parts.
>
> The first part (*Moderato e Molto Ritmato*) is preceded by a (*forte*) introduction featuring some of the thematic material. Then comes a three-part contrapuntal episode leading to a second theme. The first part finishes with a recurrence of the first theme combined with fragments of the second.
>
> A solo clarinet cadenza leads to a middle part, which is in the plaintive mood. It is a gradually developing canon in a polytonal manner. This part concludes with a climax based on an ostinato of the theme in the canon, after which a sudden change in tempo brings us back to the rumba dance rhythms
>
> The finale is a development of the preceding material in a stretto-like manner. This leads us back once again to the main theme.
>
> The conclusion of the work is a coda featuring the Cuban instruments of percussion.

The note is more of interest for what it reveals of Gershwin's progress into the more sophisticated areas of musical terminology — certainly more sophisticated than he had been used to hitherto — with mention of 'contrapuntal episode', 'cadenza', 'polytonal manner', 'ostinato', 'canon', 'stretto' and 'coda'. This was not done merely so as to impress, since the première of the work was to be given at what was essentially a popular occasion. What is likely is that at this time Gershwin was particularly under the influence of

Joseph Schillinger, with whom he studied for about four and a half years. In February 1936 Gershwin gave Schillinger a signed photograph, on which he wrote: 'In appreciation of his great talent as a teacher and with all my best wishes.'

Schillinger's own view of the relationship, as given in 1940, was that Gershwin:

> . . . was at a dead end of creative musical experience. He felt his resources, not his abilities, were completely exhausted . . .
>
> When we met, Gershwin said: 'Here is my problem: I have written about seven hundred songs. I can't write anything new any more. I am repeating myself. Can you help me?' I replied in the affirmative, and a day later Gershwin became a sort of 'Alice in Wonderland'.
>
> Later on he became acquainted with some of the materials in this book [Schillinger's own] . . . 'You don't have to compose music any more — it's all here,' he remarked.

But there is no indication that there was any fundamental change in Gershwin's approach to composition, despite the acquisition of technical terms, certainly not in *Cuban Overture*, as it became. There is still the repetition, both of melody and rhythm, and a lack of musical development of the material. Even the melodic interest is not especially inspiring. The best one can say for the work is that the orchestration has a clarity of texture that is welcome, and which may have been due to Schillinger's influence, and that it has some interesting chromaticism at times.

But on a purely material plane, the concert in which the overture received its first performance was a landmark in that it was the first all-Gershwin concert, and drew a huge crowd to the Lewisohn Stadium. Gershwin himself was the soloist in *Rhapsody in Blue* and in the *Second Rhapsody*, with Albert Coates conducting the Philharmonic. The *Concerto* was played by Oscar Levant, with Bill Daly conducting, and the rest of the programme included *An American in Paris* and, of course, the *Rumba*, which changed its title later that year when Gershwin played in a benefit concert at the Metropolitan Opera House on 1 November for the Musicians' Symphony, which was an orchestra consisting of two hundred unemployed musicians. It was during rehearsals for this concert, incidentally, that Allan Lincoln Langley made his assertions about Gershwin's basic ability as a composer, as we have already seen.

126

For Gershwin, however, the Lewisohn Stadium concert had been a new high point in his career, as he wrote to George Pallay the day after:

It was, I really believe, the most exciting night I have ever had, first, because the Philharmonic Orchestra played an entire program of my music, and second, because the all-time record for the Stadium concerts was broken. I have just gotten the figures: 17,845 people paid to get in and just about 5,000 were at the closed gates trying to fight their way in — unsuccessfully.

There is something faintly distasteful in the gratification Gershwin derived from the thought of 5,000 people fighting to get in to hear his music — and failing to do so. But it was as well for him to savour the success of 1932, because initially 1933 was to be a very different matter.

Pardon My English opened at the Majestic Theater on 20 January 1933 and closed after 46 performances. Of course it was a time of great difficulty for the theatres in America, and it is thought that about two-thirds of the New York theatres alone had closed by 1931 through lack of business. Under President Roosevelt, as part of the New Deal, the Federal Theater Project was set up in 1935 to give employment to actors, singers, musicians and other sorts of entertainer, and by 1939, when it was wound up by Congress, it had employed more than 12,000 people. Early 1933 was not, therefore, the best time to be associated with a theatrical disaster, and in fact the Gershwins had not wanted to be involved with *Pardon My English*. For one thing, they did not like the central character — who becomes a thief as a result of blows to the head and is finally cured by the same means — nor the book, which was not in a finalized state when they began working on it, and had several hands mixed up in it before it was finished, which of course necessitated changes to the score.

The Gershwins only became engaged on it because of their sense of loyalty to Aarons and Freedley, who had lost their Alvin Theater the previous year (1932), and who said that unless the Gershwins agreed to write the score, the show would lose its backers and that would be the end of Aarons and Freedley as a team. Gershwin felt particularly concerned for Aarons, since he had produced his first

127

full-scale musical, *La, La, Lucille*, in 1919. But his premonitions about the basic viability of the idea would not go away, and were not helped by the disastrous out of town experience during the pre-New York run. Jack Buchanan, who had been engaged to play the lead, bought himself out of the show in Boston, and was reputed to have paid $20,000 to do so, though Ira Gershwin subsequently admitted that this was probably an exaggeration.

Despite the announcement in advance that there would be a top price of three dollars for the seats in the theatre, and that Gershwin himself would conduct on the opening night, *Pardon My English* did not recoup the fortunes of Aarons and Freedley. That was the end of the partnership, and Freedley even had to leave the country for a time in order to escape his creditors. It was only a temporary setback as far as he was concerned, however, for in 1934 he returned with the smash hit of Cole Porter's *Anything Goes*, and in 1936 he had another Cole Porter hit with *Red, Hot and Blue*, starring Ethel Merman, Jimmy Durante and Bob Hope. He remained active on Broadway until 1950, and then became involved with charitable and administrative work in the theatre, only dying in 1969 at the age of seventy-seven.

Things did not turn out so well for Aarons, however. He went on to the West Coast, and eventually was involved with Warner Brothers on the film about Gershwin, *Rhapsody in Blue*, but died from a heart attack in 1943, when he was only fifty-two, before the film was made.

Though the flop of *Pardon My English* affected Aarons and Freedley, it made little visible impression on Gershwin, and in the early part of 1933 he moved from Riverside Drive to a fourteen-room duplex apartment at 132 East Seventy-second Street. As in their previous moves, Ira and Leonore could never be far away, so they moved in across the road at 125 East Seventy-second Street, and so they worked together on their next musical, a sequel to *Of Thee I Sing* entitled *Let 'Em Eat Cake*.

It is always very tempting to capitalize on success, and when a cult figure is involved, the result may often turn out to be a box-office success, if not an artistic one, but when it is a matter of the somewhat chancy world of musicals, it ought to have been apparent that there was a huge risk involved in putting on *Let 'Em Eat Cake*.

The central subject is revolution. The running mates Wintergreen and Throttlebottom are not re-elected, and have to cede the

The bedroom of Gershwin's penthouse on Riverside Drive, where he moved in 1928. From its large terrace there were imposing views of the Hudson and the Palisades, and the severely modern style bore witness to the composer's success in life. There was also plenty of room to display his ever increasing art collection. The screen is inspired by *An American in Paris*, painted by Henry Botkin.

The Music Box Theater in New York where *Of Thee I Sing* opened on 26 December 1931 and ran for 441 performances. The show became famous as the first musical to be awarded the Pulitzer Prize, though technically it was for the book and lyrics, and not the music, because of the terms governing the award of the prize.

Rosamond Walling Tirana, a distant relation by marriage of Gershwin, and twelve years his junior, to whom Gershwin paid court for a time but never seriously seems to have considered suitable as a wife. During the years from about 1928 to 1931, however, they saw a great deal of each other when their respective careers permitted.

Leopold Godowsky senior, pianist, composer, and co-inventor of Kodak colour film, in a photograph taken by George Gershwin. His son, Leopold Godowsky junior, married Frances Gershwin, and so became the composer's brother-in-law.

Gershwin with Serge Koussevitzky in Boston for the première of the *Second Rhapsody* there in January 1932. This was effectively one of the works commissioned by the great conductor for the fiftieth anniversary of the Boston Symphony Orchestra, who gave the first performance with Gershwin as soloist.

Gershwin's talent as an artist, though by no means as great as that as a composer, was nevertheless appreciable, and his portrait of Arnold Schoenberg has a remarkable quality in its directness and impression of the other man's austerity and intelligence. Gershwin painted this self-portrait in 1932.

In 1934 Gershwin carried out a tour
with the Leo Reisman Band and the
tenor James Melton, conducted by
Charles Previn. They gave twenty-
eight concerts in twenty-eight days,
beginning in Boston and ending in
Brooklyn. The photograph was taken
in Aeolian Hall (inset is the exterior),
which had been the setting for
Gershwin's concerts with Eva Gauthier
in 1923 and Paul Whiteman in 1924,
when *Rhapsody in Blue* was first heard
there, and this tour celebrated its tenth
anniversary.

Gershwin and his artist cousin Henry Botkin at Folly Beach, South Carolina, where Gershwin stayed whilst working on *Porgy and Bess* so as to soak up the authentic atmosphere of the Deep South. The photograph was taken by Gershwin's devoted secretary Paul Mueller.

George Gershwin's sketch of the room in which he worked and slept during the five weeks that he spent on Folly Island during the composition of *Porgy and Bess*.

Gershwin did not complete *Porgy and Bess* whilst in South Carolina, but had to continue work on it after his return to New York later in the summer of 1934, and did not finish it until 23 August 1935, only three days before rehearsals were due to begin. This photograph was taken in July 1935, as he was completing the first scene of Act Three.

Gershwin, Du Bose Heyward, the author of *Porgy*, and Ira in Boston for the try-out of the opera on 30 September 1935. On another copy of this photograph which the brothers inscribed for Heyward, George wrote a musical quotation from 'A Woman is a Sometime Thing', and expressed the hope that their collaboration would be an 'always' thing. Though he did not live to see it, posterity fulfilled his hope.

Gershwin on stage at the end of the first night of *Porgy and Bess* at the Alvin Theater in New York, with the conductor, Rouben Mamoulian, behind him to the left and Heyward to the right. Todd Duncan, the first Porgy, is kneeling left.

The principal characters in the first production of *Porgy and Bess*: John Bubbles as Sportin' Life, Todd Duncan as Porgy, and Anne Brown as Bess.

A scene from the 1986 production of *Porgy and Bess* at the Glyndebourne Festival, in which the part of Porgy was played by Willard White (centre).

George and Ira Gershwin boarding the TWA plane that was to take them from Newark to Hollywood on 10 August 1936. Neither man looks particularly happy, and the composer was going in the knowledge that he had not had a success since *Of Thee I Sing*, which was followed by three commercial flops in a row.

On 9 and 10 July 1936, Gershwin played at the Lewisohn Stadium in New York on what turned out to be the last occasion he appeared before the public in the city. The first day was the hottest ever recorded in New York, which in part accounted for the relatively poor attendance, and by comparison with previous concerts there, the audiences were not at all good.

On arrival in Hollywood, the Gershwins soon got to work on *Shall We Dance*. Gershwin talks to Ginger Rogers, and Fred Astaire is on her right. Behind are Hermes Pan, dance director, Mark Sandrich, director, Ira Gershwin and Nathaniel Shilkret, musical director. The second Hollywood experience turned out to be no happier than the first, and Gershwin began more and more to regret his self-imposed exile.

One of the more unusual friendships of Gershwin's life was formed in the last months in Hollywood with Arnold Schoenberg, whose portrait he painted in December 1936. Schoenberg was generous in his appreciation of Gershwin which he wrote after his death.

One of the many names linked romantically with Gershwin's was that of Paulette Goddard, with whom the composer was photographed at Palm Springs. Despite his attraction to her, however, there is little evidence that the feeling was mutual in the way that Gershwin seemed to wish. She was in any case married to Charles Chaplin at the time, and did not divorce from him until 1941, after Gershwin's death.

Above and opposite: Gershwin conducting a rehearsal with the Los Angeles Philharmonic for two concerts on 10 and 11 February 1937. It was whilst Gershwin was rehearsing an excerpt from *Porgy and Bess* on this occasion that the first intimation of his illness appeared. He suddenly began to sway and seemed about to fall off the podium, but Paul Mueller rushed to steady him. During the performance of the *Concerto in F*, however, Gershwin had a short blackout and forgot the music — an unheard of occurrence for him. At the same time he thought he could smell burning rubber, a sensation which returned during a similar situation in April. By this time his fatal illness had begun to take its course.

George Gershwin's funeral took place in the pouring rain on 15 July 1937 at the Emanu-El Temple in Manhattan, where his body had been brought from California. Many waited outside, unable to find room in the building. On 8 August the largest crowd ever known in the history of the Lewisohn Stadium — over 20,000 — attended a memorial concert.

White House to John P. Tweedledee. John and Mary Wintergreen borrow money from Throttlebottom and start up a business making blue shirts on Union Square in New York. Things do not go very well at first, until the Wintergreens realize that if their shirts were worn by those who go to Union Square to argue and agitate, they could form a whole Blue Shirt army, and engineer a revolution, take over the government, and so get back into power. The services of Kruger, a professional agitator, are enlisted, and eventually a fascist Blue Shirt state is set up. War debts that remain unpaid by foreign states are now called in, and when they refuse to pay, a baseball match is arranged between the representatives of those states and the Supreme Court. The hapless Throttlebottom is detailed as umpire, and when he makes the mistake of ruling for the opposition, he is pronounced a traitor by the revolutionaries and sentenced to be guillotined. He is only saved — as Wintergreen was in *Of Thee I Sing* — by the appearance of Mary who, with the help of her friends, organizes a dazzling fashion show which distracts the mob from their bloody intentions. Throttlebottom lives to become President, democracy returns to America, and the Wintergreens return to shirt-making.

Let 'Em Eat Cake opened at the Imperial Theater in New York on 21 October 1933, and ran for only ninety performances. The critic of *Newsweek* pronounced that it was 'dull and dreary', and Brooks Atkinson said that the authors of the libretto had allowed their hatreds to triumph over their sense of humour.

Unfortunately, the score did not impress in the way that it had for *Of Thee I Sing*, and Gershwin made some rather pretentious claims for it that did not help its cause:

> I've written most of the music for this show contrapuntally, and it is this very insistence on the sharpness of a form that gives my music the acid touch it has — which points the words of the lyrics, and is in keeping with the satire of the piece. At least, I feel that it is the counterpoint which helps me do what I am trying to do.

There is a curiously vague, even pleading note, which rings oddly when compared with so many of the previous Gershwin pronouncements, and despite the fact that there was no financial crisis in Gershwin's life, when one takes such evidence as the claims of Joseph Schillinger into account also, there certainly seems to have been some sort of crisis in Gershwin's artistic life.

In fact, Rouben Mamoulian, eventual producer of *Porgy and Bess*, who first met Gershwin this year at the Corner Club in Rochester, along with Artur Rubinstein, Eugene Goossens and others, felt it instinctively. As he put it:

[My] first impression of Gershwin during that evening was that of a rather worried and anxious young man — very ambitious and not very happy. Rather reserved and self-centered and in some curious way suspicious of the world, looking not unlike a child with more apples than he can comfortably hold in his hands and afraid that someone would take them away from him.

One begins to detect, in the photographic portraits of Gershwin from now on, a deep sense of something sad and remote behind the successful façade.

In December of that year (1933) Gershwin went down to Florida, to stay with Emil Mosbacher in Palm Beach, where he worked on the 'I Got Rhythm' Variations for piano and orchestra. This was to be a new piece to feature in an American tour he was planning, celebrating the tenth anniversary of *Rhapsody in Blue*, to start on 14 January in Boston, and end in Brooklyn on 10 February, giving twenty-eight concerts in as many days. The orchestra on the tour was to be the Leo Reisman 'Symphonic Orchestra' according to the programme, though the orchestra was not the permanent Reisman ensemble, simply an *ad hoc* group given his name. Nor did Reisman himself take part, since he broke a hip and had to be replaced by Charles Previn (the uncle of André Previn), who had worked with Gershwin before, as far back as *La, La, Lucille* in 1919, and more recently in *Of Thee I Sing*. The tenor James Melton also took part in a programme that opened with the *Concerto in F*, then a group of orchestrated Gershwin songs, followed by three solos from James Melton. The first half ended with *Rhapsody in Blue*, and the second half opened with *An American in Paris*. James Melton then sang a second group of songs, followed by the 'I Got Rhythm' Variations, an orchestral version of 'Wintergreen for President' from *Of Thee I Sing*, and a medley of Gershwin songs at the piano to close.

By this time — and possibly from as early as 1931 — Gershwin had engaged Paul Mueller as a kind of secretary. Recommended by Kay Swift, in whose judgement Gershwin had complete confidence,

Mueller stayed with Gershwin to the end. He had, as he saw it, three main functions on this tour. The first was to look after all the band's instruments, and see that they were loaded on and off the special train which Gershwin had hired, and reached the concert hall safely. The fact that there were more than fifty musicians, and that the leader had a Stradivarius, made this no light task. Gershwin himself had a heavy practice keyboard which only Mueller was allowed to handle, and never any less than four bags with him. Since they passed through more than forty cities, according to Mueller's calculations, the number of times that confusion might have ensued were legion. But he also had other duties, which included giving Gershwin a daily massage, since he was unable to take any other form of exercise whilst they were on tour, and — by no means any less important — keeping at arm's length the importunate females who mobbed not only Gershwin, but Melton as well.

Unfortunately, the tour was not the financial success that Gershwin had expected, and he had to pay $5,000 out of his own pocket to make good the losses incurred. As Gershwin himself put it: 'The tour was a fine artistic success for me and would have been splendid financially if my foolish manager hadn't booked me into seven towns that were too small to support such an expensive organization as I carried.' It is a sad comment that the 'foolish manager' was none other than Harry Askins, who had done so much all those years ago to interest Max Dreyfus in Gershwin.

Despite the tour's lack of financial success, Gershwin maintained that it was a worthwhile thing for him to have done, and he had seen cities that he had not visited before. And then, he was working so hard at this time that he was quickly immersed in another venture. Just over a week after his final concert, he began a radio programme in New York entitled *Music by Gershwin*, which went out every Monday and Friday evening from 7.30 for fifteen minutes, starting on Monday, 19 February. His salary was said to be $2,000 a week, and there was a certain irony in the fact that the programme was sponsored by Feen-A-Mint, the chewing-gum laxative, in view of Gershwin's trouble with constipation.

But he soon found that the two fifteen-minute programmes twice weekly were considerably more demanding than playing the same programme night after night — even for twenty-eight consecutive nights, as he had on the tour, and on 4 March (1934) he was quoted in the *New York Times* as saying that, because radio involved preparing an entirely different programme for each broadcast, it did not take long to exhaust even an extensive repertoire. As he put it: 'The microphone is like a hungry lion the way it eats up material.' And he went on: 'It's really liable to prove something of a strain even to a composer who is in the habit of turning out melodies more or less on schedule. And I've written close to a thousand songs.' Even so, he continued with the programmes on a regular basis until 31 May, and then started up again on 23 September until 23 December (1934) but then with a thirty-minute show once a week.

In private he was hurt by the adverse criticism he received and said to Harold Arlen: 'What do they want me to do? What are they criticizing me for?' As Arlen pointed out, there was still the Depression, and what Gershwin did on those radio shows may well have helped himself, but it also helped a good many of the members of the profession, too. In his more defiant moods Gershwin would point out that without Feen-A-Mint he would not have been able to write *Porgy and Bess*, and that was now becoming a reality at last. In a rather wry comment, it was the author of *Porgy*, DuBose Heyward, who rationalized the way in which artists such as Gershwin and himself had to resort to the help of commerce to assist the creative process: 'There is, I imagine, a worse fate than that which derives from the use of a laxative gum. And, anyhow, we felt that the end justified the means.'

8 PORGY AND BESS: I

Porgy and Bess:
I

All artists are liable to find perpetual exposure to public approval or disapproval a lacerating experience, since outright condemnation is bad, but it is even worse to achieve success, and then experience rejection after that. Of course some artists are able to cultivate a protective layer about them and pursue their careers regardless, but there must inevitably be moments of questioning, even so, and the possibility that not all the critics can be wrong all of the time.

Gershwin had certainly given the impression, as he rose to fame and popularity, that he had his own protective layer, and indeed that he was the one capable of being lacerating on occasions. But as more became expected of him, he had to fall back more and more on his own resources which, to the outside observer, must have seemed inexhaustible. Yet at times he also seemed to be getting out of his depth, and unable to stop himself. He gave out for popular consumption naive and egocentric remarks which only made him look foolish. One of the most profound things that he was able to say about Schubert, for example, was that if he had been living in Gershwin's day he would have been well-off and comfortable. Or about composers in general: 'Not many composers have ideas. Far more of them know how to use strange instruments which do not require ideas.'

There must have been considerable anxiety and insecurity, and there is little doubt that as Gershwin approached the most substantial work of his life, he had never been less mentally and emotionally equipped to undertake it. Nor technically, for that matter, in view of his minimal amount of training. And of course the fact remains that Gershwin was highly sensitive to criticism,

and the actress Kitty Carlisle, who saw quite a lot of him at this
time, put her finger on it:

> He had everything, but there was something terribly vulner-
> able about him. People felt very protective about him. Why I
> don't know. He was successful, he was good-looking, women
> adored him, he had money. He had everything, but yet there
> was something vulnerable, childlike. He needed approval.
> Yes, maybe that's it. And you felt it. That was part of his
> charm. Enthusiasm — that was part of his charm too. And his
> enthusiasm was terribly boyish for a man who was that
> successful.

Under this charm and enthusiasm there was, then, the vulnerabil-
ity, and during 1934 Gershwin decided to undergo psychoanalysis
with Gregory Zilboorg (1890–1959), who had treated several
famous and wealthy clients. During the year or so that Gershwin
was a patient of Zilboorg he saw him five times a week for an hour,
except when prevented from doing so by unforeseen circumstances
or clashes of engagements. Towards the end Gershwin complained
that he did not feel that he was deriving the hoped-for benefit from
the sessions, and that he was being drawn out much more than he
had anticipated. Of course Zilboorg never betrayed Gershwin's
confidences out of ethical considerations, and Gershwin himself
never revealed precisely what had alarmed him, but when Zilboorg
spoke to a conference in New York not long before he died, he
indicated in the broadest terms the nature of Gershwin's neurosis
— at least by implication. He said that most creative people are
afraid to be treated because they cherish an unknown inner
something which they are afraid to expose to the world or indeed
have touched by anyone. They feel they are in danger of destroying
the very source of creativity. This could also explain Gershwin's
reluctance, or indeed inability, to form a close emotional attachment, and the relationship with his parents in early life must also
have played its part in creating or exacerbating the problem.
Analysis can be a very destructive experience for some, and
perhaps Gershwin saw the implicit danger ahead, and so withdrew.
Or his instinct for self-preservation asserted itself in time. Of course
it was a period when psychoanalysis became very fashionable for
the sort of people who moved in Gershwin's circle, and it was also
somewhat predictable that in the end he should decide that it was

not worth it. But perhaps, too, he had found the thing that he had hankered after for so long, and that was to be the last major work of his career, the opera *Porgy and Bess*.

After initial contacts with the author of *Porgy*, DuBose Heyward, Gershwin had never lost sight of the possibility of turning it into an opera, but for one reason or another he never got round to it. However, after the premières of the *Second Rhapsody* in the early part of 1932 and the successful launch of *Of Thee I Sing* on Broadway, Gershwin's mind once more turned to the opera, and on 29 March he wrote to Heyward:

My dear Mr. Heyward,

I am about to go abroad in a little over a week, and in thinking of ideas for new compositions, I came back to one that I had several years ago — namely, *Porgy*, and the thought of setting it to music. It is still the most outstanding play that I know, about the colored people. I should like very much to talk with you before I leave for Europe ... Is there any chance of your being abroad in the next couple of months? I hope this letter finds you and your wife in the best of health, and hoping to hear from you soon, I am

Sincerely yours,
George Gershwin.

In the event Gershwin did not go abroad at that time, as we have already seen, largely because Morris Gershwin was ill, and eventually died on 15 May 1932. And that smoothed matters for Heyward, who warmed to the idea once more with enthusiasm: 'I would be tremendously interested in working on the book with you. I have some new material that might be introduced, and once I got your ideas as to the general form suitable for the musical version, I am pretty sure that I could do you a satisfactory story.'

Disappointingly for Heyward, however, Gershwin had to write and tell him on 20 May 1932, that he was so busy that he saw no possibility of writing the opera before the following January. In the meantime, however, he suggested that they should meet, either in New York or at Heyward's home, at least a number of times, before any real work started on the music. There was also a practical angle to it from Gershwin's own side, in that he needed more time to familiarize himself with the story. It was some time since he had

137

read it: 'I shall be around here most of the summer, and will read the book several times to see what ideas I can evolve as to how it should be done. Any notions I get I shall forward to you.'

There matters might well have rested for some time, for during the summer of 1932, as we saw earlier, Gershwin was busy with *Cuban Overture* and the Lewisohn Stadium concert. However, in September Heyward wrote to Gershwin and informed him that Al Jolson was now interested in *Porgy* as a vehicle for himself, and had made approaches in order to find out what the situation would be in relation to copyright. Heyward himself was not too enthusiastic about the Jolson idea, and clearly preferred Gershwin, but he was well aware that *Porgy* represented a property — 'an asset', as he put it — 'and in these trying times this has to be considered.' What Heyward proposed, therefore, was that there should be a contractual agreement between himself, Gershwin, and his producer, so that he had a firm legal base from which to operate and so feel in a much stronger position to negotiate with Jolson:

> Therefore, before I turn this [the Jolson idea] down flat, I think we should execute the customary agreement with your producer, with whom, I presume, you have already been discussing the matter . . . It seems to me that this is very important for both of us, as certainly neither of us would wish to put our time on it without this protection.

Heyward showed himself to be as businesslike and practical as Gershwin himself could be when once he went into production:

> Will you please at the earliest possible moment wire me whether your associates are prepared to enter into a definite agreement at this time, so that I may know how to handle the Jolson matter. I will then leave promptly for New York so that we may get that settled, and also have our first conference on the rewriting of the book.

Heyward also made the suggestion, which came out almost as an afterthought, that they might avoid the whole dilemma by using Jolson for their version, and coming to some sort of agreement with him. He admitted, however, that he realized that Gershwin might find it 'too preposterous'.

Gershwin envinced no sort of alarm or dismay in his reply. He was not going to be rushed into anything. As far as he was concerned, nothing that Jolson could do would conflict with his own vision of what the opera would be. Of course Jolson was 'a very big star, who certainly knows how to put over a song', Gershwin admitted, but as he told Heyward, 'the sort of thing I had in mind for *Porgy* is a much more serious thing than Jolson could ever do'. There was, as then became clear, a very practical aspect to the matter from Gershwin's own point of view. Writing *Porgy* would for him be 'more a labor of love than anything else'. He knew that it would be difficult to turn the projected opera into the sort of money-spinner that his shows had often been in the past, and it seems as if even at this point he was determined that there would be no blacking-up in his version; he had set his heart on an entirely black cast. All things considered, therefore, he advised Heyward that if he were able to make money out of a collaboration with Jolson, he ought to go ahead: 'If you can see your way to making some ready money from Jolson's version, I don't know that it would hurt a later version done by an all-colored cast.' As then became clear, Gershwin had no producer in mind, so he could not respond positively to Heyward's request for a binding agreement, if he had wanted to do so at that moment. But he was able to give as his reason the explanation that he wanted to write the work first, and then see which producer would be best for it.

Even when, the following month (14 October 1932), Heyward's agent informed Gershwin that Jerome Kern and Oscar Hammerstein II were now discussing with Jolson the possibility of writing *Porgy*, the composer still refused to be forced into committing himself to Heyward. So far as Gershwin was concerned, Jolson could have the rights, because his version would simply be adding songs to the play that Heyward wrote, whereas Gershwin envisaged a very different treatment of it. Again he stressed that he did not want to stand in the author's way if he wanted to make some money out of his 'property'. Heyward had in fact admitted to Gershwin that he was 'in a fairly tight spot' as far as money was concerned, and he was at pains to assure him that he had no intention of working on a musical with Jolson, Kern and Hammerstein, but merely of selling the story to them. Gershwin could afford to be magnanimous, since he was not having to commit any of his money, and he felt that there was going to be no real competition in any case from the rival team. Somewhat touchingly, therefore, Heyward found Gershwin's attitude to the whole business 'simply splendid', and writing on 17 October 1932, he said: 'It makes me all the more eager to work with you some day, some time, before we wake up and find ourselves in our dotage.' In this way Gershwin obtained a moral and emotional commitment from Heyward without having to bestir himself at all, and a potentially tiresome matter resolved itself, seemingly to everyone's satisfaction.

More than a year went by, but eventually contracts were signed with the Theatre Guild on 26 October 1933, and as soon as various legal details had been dealt with, a public announcement was made on 3 November that the Guild would produce a musical version of *Porgy*. As Heyward put it:

> We had hoped, and it was logical that the Theatre Guild would produce the opera. An excursion into that field of the theater was a new idea to the directors. But then they had gambled once on *Porgy* and won. There was a sort of indulgent affection for the cripple and his goat on Fifty-second Street. Most certainly they did not want anybody else to do it, and so contracts were signed.

At long last Heyward was in the position that he had always wanted to be in — namely, being able to get down to work in the secure knowledge that it would not be wasted effort, and on 12 November 1933 Heyward wrote to Gershwin to tell him that he had been doing some fairly concentrated work on the play. In particular he envisaged a completely different opening scene, and one which, incidentally, very much appealed to Gershwin, and which he turned into the Jasbo Brown piano sequence, so often cut from productions subsequently:

> I am offering a new idea for opening of scene as you will see from the script. The play opened with a regular riot of noise and color. This makes an entirely different opening, which I think is important. What I have in mind is to let the scene, as I describe it, merge with the overture, almost in the sense of illustration, giving the added force of sight and sound. I think it would be very effective to have the lights go out during the overture, so that the curtain rises in darkness, then the first scene will begin to come up as the music takes up the theme of jazz from the dance hall piano. The songs which I have written for this part will fall naturally into the action and mood of the separate flashes of Negro life.

140

This was an example of an idea of Heyward's which made a positive contribution to the conception of the opera, but there were others that were less happy. For instance, Heyward felt that there should be no recitatives, and was in favour of something much more akin to the genuine *opéra comique*, that is, with spoken dialogue. He felt that it would give the work speed and tempo. He went on:

> This will give you a chance to develop a new treatment carrying the orchestration through the performance (as you suggested) but enriching it with pantomime and action on the stage, and with such music (singing) as grows out of the action. Also, in scenes like the fight, the whole thing can be treated as a unified composition drawing on lighting, orchestra, wailing of crowd, mass sounds of horror from people, etc. instead of singing.

Gershwin hedged in his reply of 25 November, saying that 'there may be too much talk' and admitting that he had not begun composing, but he said that he wanted to think a great deal more about it, and devote more time to 'the gathering in of thematic material before the actual writing begins'. In this respect Gershwin was extremely wise, since he had had no first-hand experience of the South at all, and his knowledge of the ways of blacks was very much limited to what he had observed in and around New York. It was providential, as it happened, that Heyward then extended an invitation to Gershwin to go and visit him in Charleston, and since Gershwin was already planning to go to Florida on a visit with Emil Mosbacher, on 2 December, he would be able to stay for two or three days in Charleston first. In his reply Gershwin specifically asked Heyward to arrange to spend most of the time with him and visit the town, so that he could hear some spirituals and visit some cafés.

According to Mosbacher, he also visited a brothel in Charleston, and that was at a time when Gershwin had talked to Mosbacher about Kay Swift and marriage, and Kay Swift had talked to Mosbacher about Gershwin and marriage — and he gave the same answer to both, namely, that he wasn't going to open his mouth. He was not, he said, 'that crazy'. One may speculate about Gershwin's expedition to the brothel. From a very basic point of view, Charleston was far removed from New York, where Gershwin was more likely to be recognised, but there may also have been simply the need or desire to explore his sexuality. For despite all the opportunities presented to him — by all accounts — he seems to have taken remarkably little advantage of them. Tales of him in bed with two women simultaneously simply do not accord with the image of the fastidious, even prudish man who was always so much in control of his person. Despite all the tales of the women whose favours he was supposed to have enjoyed, remarkably little concrete evidence exists. In Hollywood there was Elizabeth Allan and the French actress Simone Simon, who was supposed to have given Gershwin a gold-plated key and holder (with the initials G.G.) to her Los Angeles home, and it was said that after Gershwin's death his mother found such a key and holder set with sapphires among the items he had left in her apartment. To be given a key is one thing, to use it, however, is quite a different matter. In short, if Gershwin were the Don Juan he was made out to be, many more women would surely have gone on record as having been his victims. Gershwin returned to Charleston on his way back from Florida to New York, on 2 January (1934), and two such visits at such an early point in the genesis of the work must have been of enormous benefit to Gershwin.

Returning to New York, Gershwin was interviewed for the *Herald Tribune*, which quoted him on 5 January, whilst describing him as 'an eager student of Negro music'. Gershwin said that 'though of course I will try to keep my own style moving in the opera, the Negro flavor will be predominant throughout'. The question of what really constituted 'Negro flavor' or Negro music, for that matter, was to be one of the great subjects for debate when the work was finally presented, but for the time being Gershwin was to have his say on the matter: 'I'd like to point out that Negro music is the prototype of jazz. All modern jazz is built up on the rhythms and melodic turns and twists which came directly from Africa. Even the rumba.' Another point to emerge from the interview was that Gershwin was hoping that Paul Robeson would take the part of Porgy.

It is interesting that when Gershwin returned from his tour early in 1934 he saw a production of Virgil Thomson's opera *Four Saints in Three Acts* with an all-black cast, which proved to him that the idea could work, and also that there would be suitable singers available when it came to casting their own work: 'The libretto was entirely in [Gertrude] Stein's manner, which means that it had the effect of a five-year-old child prattling on. Musically, it sounded early 19th century, which was a happy inspiration and made the libretto bearable — in fact, quite entertaining. There may be one or two in the cast that would be useful to us.' It was amazing how patronizing Gershwin could be at times where other artists were concerned. That he should not care for either Gertrude Stein or Virgil Thomson was one thing, but when he condemned them in terms of reference which one suspects were far from self-determined on his part, one feels at the very least that he was missing something of artistic significance at a time when American creative writers and composers were making themselves heard in their own — and not any other — way.

One feels at times that some of Gershwin's statements were almost intended as a kind of sympathetic magic; that if he articulated the thought, it would become reality. On another occasion, after the opening of *Porgy and Bess*, he said that he hoped that the Metropolitan would mount it, with Lawrence Tibbett in the role of Porgy. Despite the fact that such a production would have necessitated the very thing that Gershwin wanted to avoid from the start — blackface performers — he must surely have realized that an opera house devoted to the classical repertoire gives at best only a handful of performances of a work during any one season, whereas almost any other theatre would be geared to what might turn out to be a long run. Of course, there would have been the status attached to such a performance, and an accolade that Gershwin would dearly have liked. In reality, the possibility of such a thing happening faded for ever when Otto Kahn died on 29 March 1934, for with his passing went much of Gershwin's influence — such as it was — at the Metropolitan.

At the end of the previous month, on 26 February (1934), Gershwin had written to Heyward to tell him: 'I have begun composing music for the first act, and I am starting with the songs and spirituals first.' In fact, the first song he wrote for the opera was 'Summertime', for which Heyward wrote the words himself. This was all very well, but Heyward realized that the pressures on Gershwin were considerable in New York, not least the radio broadcasts, and in a letter of 2 March (1934) although he took the opportunity to congratulate Gershwin on the programmes, at the same time he expressed his fears over progress on the opera: 'I have been hearing you on the radio and the reception was so good it seemed as though you were in the room. In fact, the illusion was so perfect I could hardly keep from shouting at you "Swell show, George, but what the hell is the news about PORGY!!!" ' Heyward then went on to tell how he had listened to a Howard Hanson opera, *Merry Mount*, that had an early American setting and because of all the advance publicity, he was afraid that their efforts would be negated. However, after listening to it on the radio, he felt that it was all very conventional, and therefore constituted no threat to them. All the same, Heyward felt that if Gershwin could spend more time down in Charleston he would drink in the atmosphere and, as a result, do a much better job on the opera in the long run: 'There is so much here that you have not yet gotten hold of.'

There was also in Heyward's case the nagging worry about money, something which no longer troubled Gershwin, and Heyward had been counting on production of the opera in the ensuing autumn (1934). When it became obvious that was not even faintly possible, Heyward signed a Hollywood contract, and wrote two screen plays for Eugene O'Neill's *The Emperor Jones* and Pearl Buck's *The Good Earth*. In April he went to New York for a conference with the Gershwins, though before that, because of other pressures — not least the Feen-A-Mint programmes — Gershwin had to admit in a letter of 8 March that composition on *Porgy and Bess* 'doesn't go too fast', and it was not until 23 May that he completed the first scene of the opera.

Just over a week later, the Feen-A-Mint programmes ceased until the autumn, and so in mid-June Gershwin left New York for Charleston, accompanied by his cousin, the artist Henry Botkin. They left by train, but Paul Mueller went ahead by car, taking all the heavy baggage with him, and was able to meet them at Charleston and drive them to their accommodation. When they had settled in, the sound of crickets at night was so loud that Paul had to go outside and bang the trees with a stick to silence them and let George get some sleep.

They did not stay in Charleston itself, but on Folly Island, a small barrier island some ten miles from Charleston, where the Heywards had a vacation home. Gershwin and Botkin rented a four-room frame cottage, which was primitive, to say the least, when compared to the usual Gershwin accommodation. As George told his mother in a letter, the nearest telephone was about ten miles away, which meant that he could work on his composition for long, unbroken stretches at a time. There were decided disadvantages, however, as he warned his mother, for the heat: 'brought out the flys [*sic*], and knats [*sic*], mosquitos [*sic*] . . . when the breeze comes in from the land there's nothing to do but scratch. If you're thinking of coming down here, consider these nuisances as I'd hate to have you make the trip and then be uncomfortable. I know you like your comforts.' A querulous Rose Gershwin would have been a disaster on Folly Island, most of all from the work point of view.

Life was not all work, however, for there were parties in and around Charleston, as well as trips for shopping and sight-seeing, so Gershwin did not get too isolated on his desert island. Nevertheless there is little doubt that this was one of the most satisfying and creative periods of Gershwin's whole career. As Heyward put it: 'to George it was more like a homecoming than an exploration. The quality in him which had produced the *Rhapsody in Blue* in the most sophisticated city in America found its counterpart in the impulse behind the music and bodily rhythms of the simple Negro peasant of the South.'

The Gullah Negroes on Folly Island and James Island had remained more detached from American culture than those on the mainland, and possibly they were nearer, as a result, to their African roots. At all events, there was a quality in their customs — especially as it affected music and rhythm in particular — to which Gershwin responded instinctively. As Heyward put it:

> The Gullah Negro prides himself on what he calls 'shouting'. This is a complicated rhythmic pattern beaten out by feet and hands as an accompaniment to the spirituals and is indubitably an African survival. I shall never forget the night when at a Negro meeting on a remote sea-island, George started 'shouting' with them. And eventually to their huge delight stole the show from their champion 'shouter'. I think he is probably the only white man in America who could have done it.

It would be a mistake, however, to imagine that the music simply flowed out of Gershwin whilst he was on Folly Island. As he wrote to Emily Paley on 22 July 1934, at times he felt lonely, and composition was certainly not effortless: 'It's been very tough for me to work here as the wild waves, playing the role of a siren, beckon to me every time I get stuck, which is often, and I, like a weak sailor, turn to them causing many hours to be knocked into a thousand useless bits.'

That was the more appealing side of Gershwin, even if the metaphor comes across as rather studied. But there was the other aspect, too, in which the same old confident, much less attractive Gershwin came to the fore. He told Heyward's wife Dorothy that the opera was 'the greatest music composed in America', and the *New York Herald-Tribune* of 8 July (1934) quoted him as saying: 'If I am successful it will resemble a combination of the drama and romance of *Carmen* and the beauty of *Meistersinger*, if you can imagine that. I believe it will be something never done before.' Be that as it may, by the beginning of November 1934 Gershwin was able to write to Heyward that he 'would like to set a tentative date for rehearsals', because he felt well enough advanced with the music to contemplate auditioning in January or February, so that the chosen cast could then start learning the music.

In fact, before the end of the year Gershwin had already found his Porgy, in the person of Todd Duncan. According to Duncan himself it was Olin Downes who had told Gershwin about Duncan, then teaching at a university in Washington. Gershwin felt instinctively that he did not want any university professor to sing in his opera, and had been going to night-clubs and listening to scores of Negro baritones, but had not found the right one. The feeling of mistrust was mutual, however, since the very name of Gershwin spelled out Tin Pan Alley to Todd Duncan, and that was, he felt, not his domain either. When Gershwin invited him to his apartment for a Sunday afternoon, Duncan said that he was unable to go, because he had a prior engagement at a little church where he was soloist. He would, however, go the following Sunday.

Gershwin himself opened the door to Duncan, and was surprised to discover that the singer had brought no accompanist. Duncan was equally surprised at the thought that Gershwin seemed unable to play for him, and so said that he would play for himself. Well, Gershwin then agreed to try. Duncan first proposed one of the old Italian arias with which many recital singers elect to open their programmes, in this case Sarti's '*Lungi dal caro bene*' from the opera *Giulio Sabino* (1781). When he announced the title to Gershwin, all he elicited from the composer was 'What?' Duncan thought that it was his Italian pronunciation that was at fault, so provided a translation. In fact, Gershwin was taken aback as much by the strangeness of the proposed song as the fact that Duncan was not offering 'Ol' Man River' or some other Negro song, as virtually all the other aspirants to the part of Porgy had done. After about eight bars Gershwin stopped and asked Duncan if he knew the song by heart, and when he answered in the affirmative, Gershwin then asked him to go and stand in front of him so that he could see him sing. Gershwin had by now memorized the opening of the aria, so that he was able to play by ear and look at Duncan. After the same eight bars Gershwin asked Duncan to be his Porgy.

The ever honest Duncan said that before he could accept the part he would need to hear the music. Gershwin laughed and said that he could arrange that, but he wanted to invite Duncan back the following Sunday, and bring along some other people, too. In a poignant moment of truth Duncan said that he would love to, but he simply could not afford to repeat the trip from Washington the following week. According to Duncan, Gershwin's immediate question was: 'Well, how much would you like?' But then he at once added: 'How much would it cost?' Duncan told him $35 or $40. Gershwin wrote out a cheque there and then, and asked Duncan if he would accept it from him. So the following Sunday Duncan again made the trip from Washington to New York, but this time took his wife with him.

That afternoon Duncan was supposed to sing three or four songs, but sang about thirty, according to his own reckoning, from opera to Negro spirituals. Then there was a pause for refreshment, and Gershwin announced that they were all going up to his workroom. Ira and Leonore came from across the street, and together the brothers Gershwin performed the whole score as then completed. As Duncan recalled: 'He and Ira stood there with their awful, rotten, bad voices and sang the whole score. Two hours we were there.' The opening music sounded like chopsticks to Duncan, who thought it awful, and turned to his wife and said: 'This stinks.' However, a further twenty minutes or so and the spell had worked for Duncan. He was caught. Nevertheless, when it came to the second act and Gershwin turned round and announced to Duncan that what followed was to be his great aria and would make him famous, the singer could hardly believe his ears as the banjo accompaniment of 'I Got Plenty o' Nuttin'' began. Gershwin's hunch was right, however, and Duncan was to sing it for the next forty years. For his Bess, Gershwin chose Anne Wiggins Brown, who had written to him requesting an audition.

On 24 January 1935, Gershwin wrote to Duncan to tell him that he was about to leave for Florida, where he would begin the job of orchestrating the opera, but that the vocal score of the first two acts would be ready before he left and would be sent to the publisher, who would let Duncan have a copy. Emil Mosbacher had rented a house at Palm Beach, so on the way down, Gershwin was able to stop briefly in Charleston on 30 January. From Palm Beach Gershwin wrote to Ira to let him know how things were getting along.

There were two chief topics of his letter to Ira, firstly the orchestration of the opera, which was going slowly, 'there being millions of notes to write', and the financing of the production. At that stage the estimated cost was $40,000, though Gershwin had been warned that costs would probably rise in time. Gershwin wanted to have a twenty-five per cent interest, that is $10,000, of which he would hold four, Ira two, and Emil Mosbacher four. However, whilst he was in Palm Beach, Gershwin heard from the Guild that the estimated cost had jumped to $75,000 or even $100,000. He was afraid that they would not want to go ahead in that case, and talked to Mosbacher about it. Mosbacher's reply was to tell Gershwin that he was willing to put up half the money needed to mount the production, and that he wanted Gershwin to go and telephone immediately to that effect. As he later confessed, he had not really wanted to invest, but that as soon as the people at the Guild knew that he was prepared to do so on that scale, then they would do anything to keep him out. He 'knew the psychology of the thing', as he put it, and that when one person makes a bid, then that creates other bids. In the long run it helped Gershwin, and probably made all the difference between doing the opera and not doing it.

Mosbacher was also a candid observer of Gershwin's working pattern. The composer worked best when he had a deadline to meet, and he would often go to parties where he would play all night, and then complain the next day when he found it difficult to work. However, Mosbacher knew that if people did not invite Gershwin to play at parties, then he would be equally difficult. Small wonder, then, that work on the orchestration of *Porgy and Bess* did not go exactly smoothly. Even after George's return to New York, it went no better, and when he wrote to Joseph Schillinger on 16 May (1935) he said that although he had finished the orchestration of the first act, and was now working on the second, 'it goes slowly', and he suggested lessons with Schillinger. Then of course there were other pressures on Gershwin, such as auditions and the engaging of the production team. Alexander Smallens was chosen as conductor. He was known to be a supporter of new music, and had conducted the performance of Virgil Thomson's opera *Four Saints in Three Acts* which Gershwin had attended. Then, for coaching the singers, Gershwin invited Alexander Steinert, himself a pianist, composer and conductor, whom Gershwin had met at a Stravinsky concert at New York Town Hall. Since Steinert had worked as vocal coach for the Russian Opera Company at that time, he was a good choice, and he had as his assistant J. Rosamond Johnson, who played Lawyer Frazier in *Porgy and Bess*. The producer was Rouben Mamoulian, who had produced the original play *Porgy*, and he temporarily left Hollywood in order to take on the opera, though he had not heard a single note of what he was to direct. What most strikes one in his account of the first occasion that George and Ira Gershwin ran through the score for him was the evident significance that the work held for both of them, and their deep need for it to be appreciated favourably.

Gershwin said, in an interview in the *New York Herald-Tribune*, that although he was very happy when the music was eventually finished, he felt 'a little empty'. It did indeed seem as if he had almost physically given birth to something, and like any proud parent, could scarcely leave his offspring alone or prevent himself from seeking approbation for it. Rouben Mamoulian told how, after a very difficult first rehearsal, he was left feeling exhausted and depressed, and when on returning to his hotel, he was told that a call was coming through from Gershwin, he hoped for some consolation and encouragement. But the call ran something like this:

> Rouben, I couldn't help calling you . . . I just *had* to call you and tell you how I feel. I am so thrilled and delighted over the rehearsal today . . . Of course I always knew that *Porgy and Bess* was wonderful, but I never thought I'd feel the way I feel now. I tell you, after listening to that rehearsal today, I think the music is so marvelous — I really don't believe I wrote it!

Later, during rehearsals, Gershwin invited Mamoulian to spend the week-end at Long Beach, 'to relax and forget *Porgy and Bess* and my music for a while'. Mamoulian did not go, but Steinert did, and when questioned as to how they spent the week-end, he replied: 'We played *Porgy and Bess* Saturday and Sunday — all day and all night.'

9 PORGY AND BESS: II

Porgy and Bess:
II

Rehearsals for the opera were due to start on 26 August 1935, and according to the last page of the orchestral score, Gershwin only finished it on 23 August, but on the first page of the orchestrated manuscript there is also 'finished 2 September,' 1935'. There were to be more changes, however, before the work reached anything like its final form.

Gershwin had had a run-through with orchestra in the middle of July, assisted by the head of CBS, William Paley. There was also a concert performance in Carnegie Hall before a small invited audience before the company went on to Boston for their out-of-town opening at the Colonial Theater there on 30 September (1935). From the Carnegie Hall performance it became apparent that the opera was very long — over four hours — and so in the week prior to the Boston opening, several things had to go, such as the 'Buzzard Song', the trio 'Oh, Where's My Bess?', and the opening piano music. Warren Munsell, Production Manager for the opera for Theatre Guild, said the opening scene had to be cut not only because of length of running time, but also because it would require a different, additional, set. Even so, according to Munsell, the production costs were still under $50,000 and that included the forty-two piece band in the pit. Generally Gershwin gave in to other, recognizably more experienced, opinion, even though it meant that some of his favourite music had to go, and others connected with the opera, such as Eva Jessye, whose choir provided the chorus, tended to feel the same way. As Eva Jessye put it:

A lot of the gutbucket stuff he particularly liked had to be cut. And, you know, he had written in things that sounded just right, like our people. For example, near the end of the opera, at the passage 'She's worse than dead, Porgy', we were doing a brush-rhythm thing with our hands, and the more long-hair people who had to do with the production cut it out.

For the character of Sportin' Life, Gershwin himself had chosen John W. Bubbles of the vaudeville team Buck and Bubbles. In the end the choice was vindicated because Bubbles produced one of the classic performances of the American stage. Problems arose, however, because Bubbles had had no classical musical training, and so had no idea how to read music, let alone stick to a written script. At times he created such chaos that it was only Gershwin's insistence that prevented him from being dropped and someone else being chosen. During rehearsals on one occasion Alexander Smallens became so angry that he stopped the proceedings and asked Bubbles if there was anything wrong with his conducting. Bubbles realized that he had upset Smallens, and so replied: 'If I had the money of the way you conduct I'd be a millionaire.'

Kay Swift recalled that on the opening night Bubbles appeared in an emerald green suit that he had provided for the show at his own expense, but which no one had seen until then. It zipped up the front, but unfortunately the zip jammed just as he was about to come on stage. His entrance music had to be played three times before he appeared. Kay Swift, seated between George and Ira, was petrified. Bubbles came on, but had to deliver the whole of 'There's a Boat Dat's Leavin' Soon for New York' with his back to the audience, and unable to stand up properly. He did it beautifully, by all accounts. Touchingly, he and his partner Buck sent Gershwin a telegram on the opening night which ran: 'May the curtain fall with the bang of success for you as the sun rises in the sunshine of your smile.'

By way of contrast, some of the black singers who had been trained traditionally had to be taught how to sing in something approaching an authentic southern dialect, and in the opinion of some critics, this use of dialect has always been one of the most questionable aspects of the opera. Obviously it has to be done supremely well in order to convince, and when the dialect is done badly, one feels that it would be better to dispense with it completely, but in some quarters the objection has been more because it appears, fifty or so years later, to be perpetuating the 'Uncle Tom' image. For better or for worse, that is how the author wrote the book, and it is not really part of the question of how well Gershwin achieved what he set out to do. Equally as important from that point of view was how much the cuts affected his initial concept of the work.

Cuts or no, the first night in Boston was well received. Francis D. Perkins, writing in the *New York Herald-Tribune*, pronounced the opera a 'notable achievement in a new field. It tells of unusually effective craftsmanship; it reflects a marked advance in Mr Gershwin's progress'. And Moses Smith, writing in the Boston *Transcript*, said that 'Gershwin must now be accepted as a serious composer'. In the opinion of the *Christian Science Monitor*, the opera was 'Gershwin's most important contribution to music'.

In New York, however, when the opera opened at the Alvin Theater on 10 October (1935), although the reviewers apportioned praise, they also made several unfavourable criticisms, and it ran for only 124 performances. There was then a tour which began in Philadelphia on 27 January 1936, went on to Pittsburgh and Chicago, and closed in Washington on 21 March.

Most of the reviewers made much of the distinction between opera and operetta, and decided that Porgy and Bess was neither one nor the other, though they were perfectly willing to concede that there were 'hits' in the work. So far as Lawrence Gilman, in the *Herald-Tribune*, was concerned, however, it was the hits which marred the work: 'They are cardinal weaknesses. They are the blemishes upon its musical integrity.' And Samuel Chotzinoff in the *Post* probably summed up the attitude of the majority when he wrote: '*Porgy and Bess* is a hybrid, fluctuating constantly between music-drama, musical comedy, and operetta. It contains numerous "song hits" which could be considered ornamental in any of the composer's musical shows . . . Yet they are too "set" in treatment, too isolated from the pitch of opera for us to accept them as integral parts of a tragic music-drama.' One might have observed that a fairer way to have approached the work would have been to drop the conception of opera entirely, and simply take the work as a hybrid, but that they seemed unable to do, for on the other hand there were those like Brooks Atkinson from the *Times* who judged it from the drama critic's point of view, and found the recitatives an impediment to enjoyment of the work. His musical colleague on the *Times*, Olin Downes, took the 'hybrid' line, though he did have the grace to say that Gershwin had 'not completely formed his style as an opera composer'.

The entire production costs sank without trace, and Gershwin was unable even to cover the cost of his copyists' fees. Naturally, in the end, as the individual tunes became popular, he recouped his money several times over, but it was the savage blow to his self-esteem at the opera's initial failure that hurt him — despite the lavish party given after the opening night at the Condé Nast apartment on Park Avenue and the silver tray inscribed with the signatures of his colleagues and friends. Gershwin would probably have expected all that in any case. He had hoped for something to outdo the popularity of *Of Thee I Sing* in the length of its run, but that was not to be. Of course, in terms of classical opera *Porgy and Bess* had an amazingly good run, even by today's standards, but the show had been mounted very much in the spirit of a Broadway musical — certainly by the backers, and even the Gershwins themselves — and in those terms it was a definite disaster. Despite Munsell's claims that the production had cost less than $50,000, all of the $70,000 put up by the investors was lost.

Gershwin put his views forward in an article that appeared in the *New York Times* on 20 October, 1935, but it was far too near the première of the work to have hoped for any very considered reply, and in any case Gershwin would not have been the person to provide that reply, even if it had been thought desirable. He took the line that *Porgy and Bess* was a folk opera:

> *Porgy and Bess* is a folk tale. Its people naturally would sing folk music. When I first began work on the music I decided against the use of original folk material because I wanted the music to be all of one piece. Therefore I wrote my own spirituals and folk-songs. But they are still folk music — and therefore, being in operatic form, *Porgy and Bess* becomes a folk opera.

If, by saying that he wanted the music to be 'all of one piece', Gershwin meant that the use of 'original folk material' would have destroyed or at very least impaired that hoped-for unity, one could point to several composers who had used folk material in their works without doing that, and indeed to works where the unity was actually achieved through its use. But although unity in purely musical terms was something that Gershwin may well have hankered after, he was rarely — if ever — able to achieve it, and certainly not in his orchestral and extended works. From this point

156

of view opera ought to have been a very suitable vehicle for his talents — Wagnerian principles apart — because of its succession of arias and ensembles, and the very episodic nature of the medium.

However, Gershwin's standpoint was in reality much less sophisticated. He rejected genuine folk music because he wanted to write his own 'spirituals and folk-songs', which he could do well enough, for song-writing was his supreme ability, but although tunes such as 'I Got Plenty o' Nuttin' ' have superficial 'folk' atmosphere, it is never more than a superficial one, and Gershwin created an ersatz folk music, which only pays lip service to real folk music. The musical profiles of tunes like 'Summertime' and 'It Ain't Necessarily So' owe much more to the commercial blues and jazz music that Gershwin had grown up with in New York, and at moments of high emotion, as in 'Bess, You Is My Woman Now', the harmony and the chordal progressions become those of the classical Western European tradition. And indeed this is true of a great deal of the music in the opera — which is not to dismiss it out of hand, of course, but simply to point out where its real roots were, and indeed, if Gershwin had thought about it, he might well have been able to acknowledge that. So the purely musical aspect ought to be distinguished from the overall content of the opera. When he went on to claim that he was doing something new in *Porgy and Bess* his claim was quite a valid one — though not from a musical point of view, but from the general concept:

> Because *Porgy and Bess* deals with Negro life in America it brings to the operatic form elements that have never before appeared in opera and I have adapted my method to utilize the drama, the humor, the superstition, the religious fervor, the dancing and the irrepressible high spirits of the race. If, in doing this, I have created a new form, which combines opera with theater, this new form has come quite naturally out of the material.

Taken in these terms, then, much of what Gershwin claimed was true. He said that the opera had entertainment value because the 'Negros, as a race, have all these qualities inherent in them', and he made a particularly good point about the character of Sportin' Life, who might well have been portrayed as a sinister and evil character — which is what he is, since he is a dope-peddler — but instead he is a 'humorous dancing villain who is likeable and believeable and at the same time evil'.

So far as the 'hit-song' element in the opera was concerned, Gershwin was on rather more dangerous ground, since that was what much of the hostility from the critics had been directed at, and which was the strongest legacy from his Broadway career. He claimed that 'nearly all of Verdi's operas contain what are known as "song hits". *Carmen* is almost a collection of song hits.' In the latter reference he was nearer the mark than he possibly knew, since in its original *opéra comique* form Bizet's *Carmen* had spoken dialogue, and therefore what Gershwin referred to as the 'song hit' element would have been even more apparent. There is also more than a tangential interest in the fact that *Carmen* was turned into a highly successful black version which owed a great deal to the concept of *Porgy and Bess*.

Would *Porgy and Bess* in fact have been better as an *opéra comique* in the strict sense — i.e. with spoken dialogue? That had been DuBose Heyward's view from the outset, and it was something which very much troubled some of the critics, particularly those who represented plays rather than opera. Gershwin's own view was this: 'The recitative I have tried to make as close to the Negro inflection in speech as possible, and I believe my song-writing apprenticeship has served invaluably in this respect, because the song-writers of America have the best conception of how to set words to music so that the music gives added expression to the words.' For some of those critics on that opening night any recitatives would have been hard to take, especially in the vernacular, and even habitués of the opera house will admit that recitative is often better in a foreign language. When sung in the vernacular, some unfortunate things will leap across the footlights, often shattering whatever atmosphere might have been created until then. Even a composer like Benjamin Britten, famed for his sympathetic treatment in setting words, has left some regrettable moments where infelicitious turns of phrase are cruelly exposed by the music. What is much more to the point is whether the general principle of including recitative was a wise choice or not. On the one hand one comes up against the virtually insoluble conflict between words and music in opera — and after all, Strauss wrote a whole opera on the issue — and on the other is Gershwin's ability to set the words as recitative, and integrate the parts into the whole.

It is unfair to judge Gershwin entirely by the things that he said, but nevertheless if they are to be regarded as having any value at all, one must at least consider them. He claimed that: 'The reason I did not submit this work to the usual sponsors of opera in America was that I hoped to have developed something in American music that would appeal to the many rather than to the cultured few.' Presumably the 'usual sponsors' meant the Metropolitan Opera Company, but can we really believe that, since he also voiced the hope that the Metropolitan would do the opera with Lawrence Tibbett as Porgy? Would 'the many' — as opposed to 'the cultured few' — still have gone to see it there? And was not the verdict of the many ultimately that the opera was not really for them, since they allowed it to close after only 124 performances?

In the end, of course, the songs did indeed reach the many, and have become loved for themselves all over the world, but as to whether *Porgy and Bess* really works as an opera, the controversy will continue. At the very least it is a pity that Gershwin did not live to try his hand again, for one feels that opera was the medium in which his talents might well have found their fulfilment.

In November 1935 Gershwin decided to go on a trip to Mexico with his analyst Gregory Zilboorg and Edward Warburg, Director of the American Ballet School at the Metropolitan. At one point they met David Siqueiros and Diego Rivera, and Gershwin hoped that the latter would paint his portrait as a memento of the visit, but he declined to do so. Instead Gershwin drew Rivera. Although Rivera inscribed '*Encantado de poser para George*' and signed the Gershwin drawing, it is less certain that he was as enthusiastic about George's talent as an artist as George later gave people to believe. On his return to New York on 17 December on the Grace liner *Santa Paula*, Gershwin was met at the pier by the whole *Porgy and Bess* company, who had just given the seventy-fifth performance of the work. There had been no native music to inspire Gershwin in Mexico as there had been in Cuba, and he found himself quoted in the *Herald-Tribune* the following day under the headline: 'Gershwin disappointed in the music of Mexico; reports quest for fresh ideas hits snag of monotony.' Instead, Gershwin declared that he was going to interest himself in politics, especially since in Mexico he had 'talked a great deal with Diego Rivera and with his radical friends, who discussed at length their doctrines and their intentions.' In a piece of embarrassing naiveté he also added: 'I'm going to try to develop my brain more in music to match my emotional development.' What emotional development? one might well have asked.

Ira now took a vacation, and once the *Ziegfeld Follies* of 1936 opened, on which Ira worked with Vernon Duke as composer, he and Leonore left for Trinidad with Vincente Minnelli. Meanwhile, George arranged a suite from *Porgy and Bess*, which had its first performance in Philadelphia at the Academy of Music on 21 January (1936) when Alexander Smallens conducted the Philadelphia Orchestra. Then George wrote a song entitled 'King of Swing' to lyrics by Albert Stillman for a revue entitled *Swing is King*, which opened at the Radio City Music Hall on 28 May (1936). This was the only new Gershwin tune, though all the rest of the music in the revue was by him. Apart from that, there was no Gershwin composition this year until much later, when George and Ira wrote a take-off of a Viennese waltz, 'By Strauss', which was included in a Vincente Minnelli revue entitled *The Show Is On*, which opened at the Winter Garden on 25 December.

But Gershwin also appeared as a concert pianist during 1936 in St Louis, Washington, Boston and Chicago, and in New York with the New York Philharmonic once again, when, on 9 and 10 July that year, he appeared at the Lewisohn Stadium as soloist in *Rhapsody in Blue* and the *Concerto*, and the original cast gave a selection of items from *Porgy and Bess* with Alexander Smallens conducting. It was the last occasion on which Gershwin played in public in New York.

True, they had, as it turned out, chosen for the first concert the hottest day ever recorded in New York. Even so, by comparison with previous Gershwin appearances at the stadium, it seemed as if his fans had deserted him. The *New York Times* announced on the morning after the first concert: 'It was George Gershwin night at the Lewisohn Stadium, and there were empty seats in the amphitheatre last night. That is news.' It was the Duc de la Rochefoucauld-Liancourt who said, in his *Maximes supprimés*, that in the misfortune of our best friends, we find something which is not displeasing to us. The New York press and George Gershwin may not always have been the best of friends, but they had rubbed along together for a number of years. Now the knife was being turned. Gershwin had been dismayed at the small audience, but he seemed to take heart when it was pointed out to him how hot it had been. 'That's right,' he said. 'I know four friends of mine who were supposed to come, but they were overcome by the heat.'

160

It was not only the Lewisohn Stadium concert during 1936 that lacked the excitement and capacity audiences of earlier days, however, and one cannot ignore the fact that people had simply become bored with hearing *Rhapsody in Blue* and the *Concerto* time and time again. Indeed, some of the critics even said as much, and suggested that the composer should find something else to play. In Gershwin's case it would have meant writing something else to play, because, like the itinerant virtuosi of the previous century, he only played his own music. But whereas Paganini, Chopin and Liszt would have been able to play other composers' pieces, even if they rarely did, Gershwin was not, and as time had gone by had been less and less likely ever to have begun doing so. It seemed more and more as if he had come to yet another crisis in his career, that he had lost his way, and the lack of popular acclaim for something that had been so dear to him as *Porgy and Bess* was indeed a terrible blow to his self-esteem.

There were other blows too. Bill Daly died suddenly of a heart attack at the age of forty-nine on 4 December 1936, and Gershwin and Kay Swift agreed to a year's separation, during which neither would write to the other, since following her divorce, he had never been able to ask her to marry him, and she was finding it difficult to be on permanent call — and she worked extremely hard on *Porgy and Bess* for him — with no prospect whatsoever of their relationship ever being put on a permanent footing. In fact they did inform each other that they were seeing other people, but after he and Ira left for Hollywood in August that year, Kay Swift never saw him again.

When looked at from a purely commercial and professional success point of view, the last few years for Gershwin on Broadway had not been anything to shout about. In fact, far from it, for with what were effectively three flops in a row — *Pardon My English* (1933), *Let 'Em Eat Cake* (1933) and *Porgy and Bess* (1935) — anyone could be forgiven for thinking that the Gershwin era was at the very least experiencing an eclipse, if nothing worse. Of course it was a time of intense hardship for the New York theatre, but if Hollywood now seemed an El Dorado, then Gershwin had compromised himself in their eyes not only by writing an opera — which was decidedly a long-haired thing to do in Hollywood at that time — but in writing an opera that had flopped. Was he any longer capable of writing a popular hit? When Gershwin then let it be known that the asking price for a movie score was $100,000 plus a percentage of the film, it was hardly surprising that there were no takers. In the event, the Gershwins settled with RKO on 26 June for the next Fred Astaire and Ginger Rogers film, then entitled *Watch Your Step*, for $55,000 for sixteen weeks' work, with an option for a second film at $70,000 for sixteen weeks' work. On 10 August 1936, George and Ira, having put their furniture and effects into store and given up their 72nd Street apartments, flew to California.

There is a curious wryness, even bitterness, lurking on the faces of both men in the photograph that shows George and Ira posing on the steps of the plane that eventually took them from Newark, New Jersey, to Glendale, California on that day in August. Bill Daly, who saw them off, recalled that Ira seemed disappointed that the plane was so small, and Kay Swift, who had travelled separately with George in a taxi, was obsessed by the mark on his forehead caused by wearing a straw hat that was too small for him. Of such moments is the stuff of human history made.

Initially the Gershwins — George, Ira and Leonore — took a suite at the Beverly-Wilshire Hotel, and then soon rented a Spanish style house at 1019 North Roxbury Drive in Beverly Hills, with a swimming-pool and a tennis court. In Arnold Schoenberg who joined the music faculty of the University of California at Los Angeles in 1936, Gershwin found another tennis enthusiast, and he invited Schoenberg to use the court when he wanted to. They also played together, and Oscar Levant recorded an incident when the common bond of tennis was briefly dislocated by the fact that they were both, in very different spheres, musicians too. The day after there had been a performance of Schoenberg quartets, Gershwin was moved to tell Schoenberg: 'I'd like to write a quartet some day. But it will be something simple, like Mozart.' Taking the remark as an oblique reference to his own music, Schoenberg replied: 'I'm not a simple man — and, anyway, Mozart was considered far from simple in his day.' The fact remains that Gershwin had a great respect for Schoenberg, and as early as September 1933 Gershwin had given money towards some scholarships for his students at the Malkin Conservatory in Boston, where the Viennese composer taught for a while when he arrived in America in October that year. The Gershwin portrait of Schoenberg is one of the most striking of the latter, and one of Gershwin's best achievements in the medium.

In one of his rather naive moments, Gershwin wrote to Joseph Schillinger on 13 October 1936 and told him that he had been considering studying either Schoenberg or Toch, but had not as yet made up his mind. He wanted to embark on a symphonic composition, either for orchestra alone, or piano and orchestra. Since it would have been difficult to find two composers more different from each other than Schoenberg and Toch at that time — if only because of the huge output of the latter — one must assume that Schillinger was having a certain amount of amusement at Gershwin's expense when he replied: 'If I were you, I would study with Schoenberg *and* with Toch. Why not find out what the well reputed composers have to say on the subject. I think it would be a good idea to work with Schoenberg on four-part fugues and to let Toch supervise your prospective symphonic compositions.'

According to Leopold Godowsky, Schoenberg did, however, give Gershwin some hints — in response to a request — on how to compose: 'Write variations on a theme and exhaust yourself with all the variations you can find, and when you think you have nothing else to think, start all over again.' Of course it was fairly standard advice and Schoenberg began by saying that he would have given it to Gershwin or anyone else, but it had not been conspicuously successful for Gershwin in the past as an aid to composition, and it assumed, on Schoenberg's side at least, an intellectual approach to composition that was totally alien to Gershwin.

After Gershwin's death, Schoenberg was generous, however, in his praise of him:

> Many musicians do not consider George Gershwin a serious composer. But they should understand that, serious or not, he is a composer — that is, a man who lives in music and expresses everything, serious or not, sound or superficial, by means of music, because it is his native language. . . . It seems to me beyond doubt that Gershwin was an innovator. What he has done with rhythm, harmony, and melody is not merely style. It is fundamentally different from the mannerism of many a serious composer. . . .
>
> His melodies are not products of a combination, nor of a mechanical union, but they are units and could therefore not be taken to pieces. Melody, harmony, and rhythm are not welded together but cast.

Beneath the general air of approval, however, there remains the fact that when taken as a 'serious' composer in these terms, there

163

are several ways in which Gershwin's work simply does not stand up to the test, and it is very interesting that what Schoenberg said about his melodies — as just as it might be, does not contradict what one might say about Gershwin's inability to write in extended form. But then nor did the later Schoenberg. The claim for Gershwin as an innovator, however, is one worthy of more consideration, coming from such a pen.

Gershwin found that Hollywood had 'taken on quite a new color' since he was last there six years previously. He found that there were now more people in the film industry who saw things in the way of East Coast show-business people, and he therefore found it much more easy to get on with them. Then he also found many friends from the East, so that life was much more sociable. He frequently met fellow song-writers Irving Berlin and Jerome Kern, and soon established a large circle of acquaintances. Even so, there were some clouds on the horizon. There were friends and relatives who had stayed in the East, such as Mabel Schirmer, to whom he wrote on 18 September 1936, 'I miss you very much, Mabel, and wish it were possible for you to come out here. This place is full of people you know and who love you!' There were also depressing moments when 'Hitler and his gang' became the chief topic of conversation, and there was the very different pace of work out in Hollywood. Gershwin was almost always at his best when having to work to a deadline and under pressure. When working for the theatre, he saw how his songs came across on stage from the very start, and if they didn't work, then he was happy to alter them or change them for something else. In the cinema, however, he did not know until it was too late what people thought of a song, or how it came across. In this way, some songs were not used at all, or wasted in the context in which they were eventually used.

So engrained was the Gershwin work habit, however, that despite the fact that they still had not had a complete script for the Astaire–Rogers film by the end of September 1936, George and Ira worked on their own initiative. They even had a complete concept for the opening of the film, in which Fred Astaire sees on a Paris kiosk a poster with a picture of Ginger Rogers, then performing in the French capital, and immediately falls in love with her, although he has never met her. He is moved to song and dance through the streets, praising his new found love to the passers-by. The song for this sequence was 'Hi-Ho', and when Pandro Berman, the producer, and Mark Sandrich, the director, heard it, they were duly

164

impressed. The latter commented: 'This is real $4.40 stuff and I'm crazy about it.' The point about the price allocated to it was that it was then the top price for a Broadway musical. Top price or not, however, it was never used in the film, and was not published until 1978. Ira's observation was that the film's budget could not stand the cost of the sets needed for the number, estimated at $55,000 — which was more than he and his brother were to receive for the entire score.

If 'Hi-Ho' was to be consigned to oblivion, however, there were some other tunes that were not, such as 'Let's Call the Whole Thing Off', 'They Can't Take That Away from Me', 'They All Laughed', 'Slap That Bass', and the song for the new title of the film, 'Shall We Dance' — though the last was not composed until the spring of 1937, to go with the final title when the film was released on 7 May that year. These tunes showed that the Gershwins were on tip-top form, and by the end of October discussions were going ahead for more film contracts. Samuel Goldwyn was bidding for their services for a new film to start on 15 January 1937, which spurred RKO into considering the option that had been written into their contract for the Gershwins to work on the next Astaire film.

In the meantime, Gershwin could enjoy the Californian climate, and also take part in a round of concerts, starting in Seattle on 15 December, three in San Francisco on 15, 16 and 17 January 1937, also taking in Berkeley and Detroit, and a further two in Los Angeles with the Los Angeles Philharmonic on 10 and 11 February. There is, however, in one of the photographs taken in Seattle in December, that deep sadness barely beneath the smile, which never seemed far away once Gershwin left for Hollywood. It was as if he had to drive himself, though the end of one year and the start of a new one gave him an element of hope. As he wrote to Mabel Schirmer:

I am welcoming 1937. How about you? Perhaps, dear Mabel, this is our year. A year that will see both of us finding that elusive something that seems to bring happiness to the lucky. The pendulum swings back, so I've heard, and it's about due to swing back to a more satisfying state. 1936 was a year of important changes to me. They are too obvious to you to mention here. So, sweet Mabel, lift your glass high with me and drink a toast to two nice people who will, in a happy state, go places this year.

From the postcards he sent to Lou and Emily Paley and Mabel Schirmer after the San Francisco concerts in January, Gershwin was tired but happy, and pleased to be moving around, even though he had to return to work on the next Astaire film. But in Los Angeles things were not quite so rosy, and Richard Drake Saunders, writing in the *Musical Courier* of 27 February 1937, articulated what others had been thinking and even saying for some time. In the course of the two Los Angeles programmes the audiences had been treated to *An American in Paris*, *Rhapsody in Blue*, *Concerto in F*, *Cuban Overture* and *Porgy and Bess* selections. In Saunders' opinion: 'In more ways than one it was a show rather than a concert. Gershwin has a certain individual flair, and an occasional work of his on a program is all very well, but an entire evening is too much. It is like a meal of chocolate eclairs.' Saunders' wrath seems to have been aroused as much by the people who attended the concert as the music itself, which was no doubt why he was so hard on it in the event: 'It fulfils a purpose in making a certain class of people conscious of such a thing as symphonic ensemble. It was obvious that a large number had never been in the auditorium before. Anyway, they saw some movie stars.'

Hard words indeed, and it was particularly unfortunate that during a performance of the *Concerto* in Los Angeles, conducted by Alexander Smallens, we now know that the first sign of Gershwin's fatal illness became apparent. He suddenly had a mental lapse and made a mistake, which was unheard of for him. It was barely noticed, but it so disturbed him that he talked to Dr Zilboorg about it on the telephone. It seems that his mind had gone blank, and he was aware of the smell of burning rubber. Dr Zilboorg told him that the cause was more likely to be physical than psychical, and advised Gershwin to go and have a medical check. He did so in late February, but he was found to be in excellent physical shape.

Encouraged by this, he went to work on the next Astaire film, *A Damsel in Distress*, based on the P. G. Wodehouse story, but with Joan Fontaine as the feminine lead instead of Ginger Rogers. After *Shall We Dance*, Fred Astaire and Ginger Rogers had agreed to go their separate ways, though they teamed up again after only fifteen months for *Carefree* (1938), *The Story of Vernon and Irene Castle* (1939) and ten years later for *The Barkleys of Broadway*. Gershwin continued his usual round, and at a party in March given by Edward G. Robinson met Stravinsky, Chaplin, Goddard, Fairbanks and Dietrich, as he told Mabel Schirmer by letter on 19 March (1937).

He found Paulette Goddard especially attractive, and their names were linked romantically by the press. Though she was married to Charles Chaplin at the time, he asked her to leave him and marry himself. Although she divorced Chaplin in 1941, there is no evidence whatsoever to suggest that Paulette Goddard contemplated Gershwin's suggestion seriously for a moment. As happened on so many other occasions, he saw her in relation to himself, not himself in relation to her, let alone both of them in relation to each other.

Marriage had become almost an obsession with Gershwin by now. As Henry Botkin recalled:

The last year of his life was an awful year. Did you know about the awful loneliness he had? I remember once he came right out with it and said, 'Harry, this year I've GOT to get married.' Just like that. Like saying he had to write a new opera or something. The truth is George wanted the most beautiful gal, the most marvelous hostess, someone interested in music. What he wanted and demanded just didn't exist. He would have loved to have a son or a daughter or two. George was very soft. I could never get over that.

Gershwin still hankered after New York, and in the same letter to Mabel Schirmer of 19 March 1937 wrote of the possibility of a Kaufman and Hart show that he and Ira would do for New York for the following November, when work on *The Goldwyn Follies* was over — meaning the next contract for the Goldwyn film. Again writing to Mabel Schirmer in April, he mentioned the possibility of a return to New York, and in May it was once more New York, and even Europe. Todd Duncan, who went to stay with Gershwin in March whilst giving some concerts with Merle Armitage in Los Angeles, recalled that Gershwin told him that although he was making much more money out of writing music for films than ever before, he was not happy working for the cinema, and had plans for more ambitious works like *Porgy*, and had decided to return to New York within the year. In June, when Harold Arlen went to say goodbye to Gershwin before leaving for New York, Gershwin asked, 'Do you have to go? All my friends are leaving me.'

167

By this time work on *Damsel in Distress* was finished, and Gershwin had written two classics for it, 'A Foggy Day' and 'Nice Work If You Can Get It', but the teaming of Fred Astaire and Joan Fontaine did not have the same impact as Astaire and Ginger Rogers had had, even if the rest of the film had been up to the same standard. But such was the relentless pace of Hollywood, that no sooner was work finished on the one picture than work had to begin on *The Goldwyn Follies*. As he wrote to Isaac Goldberg on 12 May, the Gershwins would have liked a vacation, but it was not possible: 'We started this week on the "Goldwyn Follies", a super, super, stupendous, colossal, moving picture extravaganza which the "Great Goldwyn" is producing. Ira and I should be taking a vacation by this time, . . . but unfortunately Goldwyn cannot put off a half million dollars' worth of principal salaries while the Gershwins bask in the sunshine.' Of the music for the film, 'Love Walked In' and 'Love is Here to Stay' showed that the Gershwins had lost none of their skill, despite the fact that Goldwyn told Gershwin to write hits 'like Irving Berlin', which could hardly have endeared him to the composer; hence the somewhat sardonic reference to him in the letter above.

It was perhaps another of the many ironies in Gershwin's career that 'Love is Here to Stay' turned out to be the last song he completed. The love he had so talked about, thought about, and written about in his songs, never came his way — or if it had, he had failed to recognize it and so missed the chance for happiness, fulfilment and the emotional security and stability that he seemed to lack. Not that that would have prevented the ultimate tragedy, but there might have been more of a roundness and warmth for one who brought so much pleasure to the lives of countless thousands of people, and yet seemed to lack it so conspicuously in his own.

10 DEPARTURE

Departure

The first sign of Gershwin's fatal illness, as we have already seen, is usually taken as the moment, when, during the performance of the *Concerto* in Los Angeles in February 1937, he experienced the blackout, and the smell of burning rubber. However, Paul Mueller recalled that during a rehearsal, when Gershwin was conducting the orchestra in a section of *Porgy and Bess*, he began to sway and seemed about to fall off the conductor's rostrum. Paul was sitting in the front row of the auditorium, and was able to rush up and steady him. That was forgotten, but then came the more alarming incident at the evening performance, after which Gershwin decided to have a check-up, but nothing seemed wrong, because physically he was fit and in good shape.

There was a repeat of the giddiness in April, and again the smell of burning rubber, but reference to the medical in February gave no cause for concern. So it was not until June that it became evident that there was something seriously wrong with Gershwin. He began to have severe headaches, was often extremely irritable, and frequently very tired. But even at this stage no one seemed to think that there was any medical explanation. Of course he had always been something of a hypochondriac, particularly where his stomach was concerned, and he had recently become concerned at the rate at which he was losing his hair, and had invested in a machine which stimulated his scalp electronically, and can hardly have improved his condition. In fact, Paul Mueller wondered whether it had not aggravated it. A certain amount of complacency in Gershwin's friends could therefore be forgiven, for he was depressed, easily irritated and very restless. Perhaps it was simply a general reaction to Hollywood.

171

So it was that Gershwin went, early in June, to see the analyst Dr Ernst Simmel. He did not agree with the composer that he was simply experiencing the effects of overwork, and recommended that he consult a physician. A few days later, therefore, on 9 June, Gershwin was examined by Dr Gabriel Segall, who still failed to find anything wrong. However, when the dizziness and the headaches failed to go away, Dr Segall called in a neurologist, Dr Eugene Ziskind, but all they discovered was that one of Gershwin's nasal passages had been damaged, and this was easily traced to a childhood experience when Gershwin had been kicked on the nose by a horse.

Nevertheless, the two doctors thought it best that he should go into the Cedars of Lebanon hospital for further tests. Between 23 and 26 June, Gershwin's skull was X-rayed and his blood tested, but still nothing was revealed, and the very thing that would have indicated the real source of the trouble — a lumbar puncture or spinal tap — was rejected out of hand by Gershwin. So he returned to the house on Roxbury Drive, and for a while his condition seemed to have improved. Certainly he complained much less of his headaches, and he was able to sleep more easily. Unfortunately, this was only a temporary state of affairs, for there was definite evidence of impaired co-ordination. He found himself dropping things, spilling food and liquids, stumbling when he had to use stairs, and his piano playing was adversely affected. There had also been a frightening experience for Paul Mueller when he was driving Gershwin to an appointment with Dr Ernst Simmel. As they were driving along, Gershwin apparently opened the door on the driver's side and began to push Mueller out, so the latter said. It must have been a terrifying experience, and almost a miracle that they were not both killed. As it was, Mueller kept control of the car and was able to pull off the road. When he demanded what Gershwin thought he was doing, all he could say was 'I don't know'.

When Harold Arlen went to say goodbye to Gershwin as mentioned earlier, he took his wife and Yip Harburg, since they were going to work on a show together in New York. Arlen was amazed at the deterioration in Gershwin's condition since he had seen him a fortnight earlier. It seemed that it would be better if Gershwin could move into smaller, quieter quarters, and since the cottage that Harburg was vacating was fairly close to the Roxbury Drive house, Gershwin moved in on 4 July, looked after by Mueller and a male nurse. But things did not improve, and Gershwin became more and more unpredictable. A box of chocolates arrived, sent by a person he did not particularly like, and he simply opened the box and crushed the contents into a mass, which he then proceeded to rub over himself. Mueller then had to bath him.

A few days later, on Friday 9 July, and exactly a month since he had first gone to Dr Segall, Gershwin's condition took a dramatic turn for the worse. He played the piano for a short while in the morning, and then at about five in the afternoon he began to feel sleepy, so decided to have a rest. He fell into a sleep that turned into a coma from which he never emerged. He was taken to hospital where a neuro-surgeon examined him, and it now became clear what the source of Gershwin's illness was. It was so late in the day, however, that only immediate surgery would be of any avail. The obvious choice was Walter Dandy, of Baltimore, but he was on a yacht out in Chesapeake Bay, and could not be contacted. In the end an approach was made to the White House, and two naval destroyers were sent to find Dr Dandy on his yacht. He was taken to Newark Airport, where a plane was arranged by Emil Mosbacher to fly Dr Dandy to California. However, in the meantime another neuro-surgeon — Dr Howard Naffziger — had been located in California and flown to Los Angeles. The operation had already begun, therefore, by the time Dandy reached Newark, so a direct line was opened up for him to the hospital, so that he could follow the progress of the operation, and offer advice when possible.

Gershwin was in the operating theatre for some five hours, but he never recovered and indeed, in Dr Dandy's opinion, he would never have survived·

I do not see what more you could have done for Mr Gershwin. It was just one of those fulminating tumors. There are not many tumors that are removeable, and it would be my impression that although the tumor in a large part might have been extirpated and he would have recovered for a little while, it would have recurred very quickly since the whole thing fulminated so suddenly at the onset. I think the outcome is much the best for himself, for a man as brilliant as he with a recurring tumor would have been terrible; it would have been a slow death.

So it was that at 10.35 on the morning of Sunday, 11 July 1937, George Gershwin died.

There were two funeral services held on 15 July, one at the B'nai B'rith Temple in Hollywood, and the other in Manhattan at the Emanu-El Temple, to where Gershwin's coffin had been brought from California. Back there, the film studios came to a halt in tribute to the man who had brought his talent, through them, to the world at large, and an estimated 3,500 people filled the synagogue in New York, whilst a thousand or so waited outside in the rain. Afterwards, the burial took place at Mount Hope Cemetery at Hastings-on-Hudson in Westchester County.

Naturally, there were many of the famous present on that emotional occasion, and there were solemn words and equally solemn music, but one image in particular says a great deal about what the death of Gershwin meant to many people, and it is all the more vivid because it involved no words. After the service in the synagogue, Todd Duncan and his wife came out onto Fifth Avenue, to see a man walking, head bowed, along the white line between the lanes of traffic, which was beginning to move once more, now that the ceremony was over. Walking doggedly ahead, oblivious of everything around him, was Al Jolson.

Less than a month later, on 8 August, the largest crowd that had ever been seen in the history of the Lewisohn Stadium (20,223) gathered for a memorial concert. Though Gershwin saw his ability to hold the masses, in his lifetime, begin to slip away from him, in death he once more was able to cast his spell over them.

John Green, who arranged the songs for the film *Shall We Dance* and provided the backing orchestra for Fred Astaire's recording of them for Brunswick, made a perceptive analysis of the enormous difference between Hollywood and New York as far as Gershwin was concerned. He pointed out how, in New York, Gershwin was 'the king of the world, the man of the hour', but in Hollywood he might be invited to houses where there was no piano, or where there was a piano but they failed to ask him to play, or if there was a piano and they did ask him to play, they would not crowd round and lionize him as they did in New York. As Green went on: 'People can be cruel everywhere, but in Hollywood these qualities are heightened. People want to be around you when you're on top and they can gore you mercilessly when you're down or they think you're down.'

Green always maintained that Gershwin was as great a song-writer as ever in those last years, but he had not had a success since 1931 with *Of Thee I Sing*. By any standards that was a fair length of

174

time, but in the instant world of Hollywood it was an eternity. And Henry Botkin asserted that although Gershwin had begun by liking Hollywood, because it was all so new and different, in the end he began to be cynical — though cynicism, Botkin said, was not his usual attitude by any means. As Gershwin said to Botkin: 'Harry, look at this place — desert. Here they drill four holes and plant palm trees. Then they drill a bigger hole and install a swimming-pool. Finally, they build a still larger, deeper hole and put up a house. It's unbelievable.'

However, as Botkin realized, it was not solely the fault of Hollywood and he always suspected that it would have been the same wherever Gershwin went that was not New York. As Botkin pointed out, Hollywood made it rather worse, especially because of all the stillness and the unreality, but the basic problem was that George and Ira, Henry and his brother Ben, had all been brought up in the heart of a big city with all its noise and bustle: 'George heard that noise and he found music in it and kept on finding it until he wrote his last note.'

One thinks automatically of *Rhapsody in Blue*, *An American in Paris*, and the *Second Rhapsody*, where the pulse of twentieth-century city life informs the whole structure, and when the film *Rhapsody in Blue* was made, this was one of the aspects highlighted. Those who had known Gershwin, however, denied that he had always been in a hurry and had to make time. Doubtless there was that element, that Jewish *chutzpah*, which impelled Gershwin along, but Kay Swift, for one, denied that there was anything 'driven' about it. All she saw was the 'joyous delight' that Gershwin brought to whatever he was doing.

It was all the more sad, then, that the 'joyous delight' was so lacking in Gershwin's private life. And indeed for one who devoted so much time to thinking about matrimony, it is somewhat amazing that he never managed to find a wife or partner. True, his egocentricity was a considerable obstacle, but he knew enough married couples to have been aware that matrimony is a two-way affair, a partnership in which, although one partner may dominate in certain ways, the other is vital to the whole.

One may speculate about his sexual orientation in this regard, for he formed some deep relationships with both men and women, without ever actually having fallen in love with either, as far as one can tell. It is not inconceivable, had he lived in our more permissive days, that he would have experimented more, but given his

175

background and the age in which he lived, there were too many factors pushing him in the opposite direction. And there is no doubt that he was prejudiced about what was proper and what improper, especially concerning those nearest and dearest to him. Even by the standards of their own day, Frances Gershwin felt that he was extremely tough on her if she used what he regarded as swear-words, or let her skirt ride up above her knee.

Almost inevitably one wonders whether he had homosexual leanings, or was bi-sexual, but there is absolutely no evidence to suggest this. The fact that he does not seem to have followed through on the reputation he had as a womanizer does not mean that he had no genuine attraction to the opposite sex, though it might have been a useful cover, had he needed it, to conceal where his real interest lay. Of more significance, perhaps, in relation to his overall personality, is the implication of a certain tension in his makeup, almost as if two distinct persons inhabited the same body.

Evidently there were two sides to the man. Those who were his intimates clearly loved and admired him, but there were also those who were less intimate and had occasion to feel less than admiration for him. Even allowing for wounded *amour-propre*, there must have been several instances of gratuitous insults emerging from Gershwin's mouth, and times when his ego seemed just too much to take. But the music is there to speak for itself, and again, the reactions from varying quarters imply that it was, and is still, capable of speaking to an enormously wide range of human beings. Like George Balanchine, for example, who saw Gershwin's music as being unequivocally Russian, although the composer had never so much as set foot inside Russia, or those who have detected strong Jewish elements in Gershwin's music, and back up their claims with direct musical quotations to prove it. It would be foolish to try and deny the fact — given Gershwin's origins and early history — and it is always interesting, and even instructive, to examine the influences which formed and influenced a notable talent — but the music itself reflects the palimpsest that is America, and American culture, even richer today than it was in Gershwin's lifetime, and still being enriched.

Those who take him to task for having made himself the spokesman for black American music — and for having done, so in a patronizing way — totally ignore the question of who else would have done so, or how they would have done, otherwise let alone whether there were any black composers at that time who might have written the opera *Porgy and Bess*.

If one considers a Gershwin contemporary such as Aaron Copland, who has also given a voice to the music of the people of America, one immediately sees that the very titles of his works reflect the cultural diversity of the nation — *Vitebsk* (1929), *El Salon Mexico* (1936), *Danzon Cubano* (1942–4), *Rodeo* (1942), *Appalachian Spring* (1944) — and Copland has never disdained to write music for the people, despite being a 'classical' composer, trained in the classical tradition. Although Gershwin was given to making grandiose statements and claims about himself, his claim to have written music for his own time and the people of America is in fact a just one. Composers such as Copland and Virgil Thomson, in their generation, as well as Samuel Barber and Leonard Bernstein, have written music that blends much more cosmopolitan traditions with specifically American ones, whereas someone like Charles Ives has restricted himself to purely American inspiration. By comparison, the music of Gershwin is truly international, because his songs in particular became identified with the world of American musical shows, and then films which eventually found their way around the world and created the popular taste in music in the period of the Second World War and immediately afterwards. It became, in fact, the *vox pop* of Western civilization as a whole.

It is essentially as a melodist, therefore, that one should approach Gershwin the composer. He knew what made a popular tune a potential hit or not. He knew that his tunes had to be readily memorized, otherwise they would never catch on. Too many notes, or too sophisticated a melodic outline, were no good. In that respect, his comparison between his own art as a song-writer — or at least setter of lyrics — and that of Schubert is not quite so far fetched, on consideration, as it might at first seem. There have not been many composers in the classical tradition who have had as great a facility as Gershwin, either in setting words or in writing memorable tunes.

Having said that, however, the actual nature of the tunes, and their quality, is certainly open to question, and one must at the very least allow for a possible degeneration in purely musical terms, though when one considers the degeneration that has taken place in popular music even since the heyday of the Beatles, then Gershwin is indeed in a different realm. He had an undoubted talent for writing vocal music, of almost any sort, and there are passages in *Porgy and Bess* — and notably not some of the better known numbers — that have remarkable lyric quality. One thinks especially of the scene in Act One in Serena's room with Robbins' body, and the solo voices sometimes supported by, and at other times in sharp contrast with, the chorus, and leading up to the poignant beauty of Serena's 'My Man's Gone Now'.

Of course, the whole relationship between folk music and art music is a vexed one, and Gershwin wrote some rather naive things about it for a book edited by Henry Cowell (1897–1965), *American Composers on American Music*, published in 1933. Henry Cowell had given Gershwin lessons from time to time over a period of about two years from 1927, and got to know him fairly well. What Gershwin wrote on that occasion fitted in well with Cowell's own view of things about American musical traditions, and their place in a truly American music of the twentieth century. In his own tastes, Cowell was much more in the tradition of Ives than Copland or Barber, but in his contribution Gershwin put forward not only a word for Southern mountain songs, country fiddling and cowboy songs, but also for ragtime, Negro spirituals and blues, and of course jazz.

Time has proved Gershwin wrong about the potential synthesis, in the hands of the proper composer, between jazz and symphonic music — though if anyone achieved it, it was himself — and also about his initial premise that the great music of the past in other countries has always been built on folk music. But insofar as he was encouraging a truly American music, one can only applaud his aims. Indeed, one may look back on the history of American music and see those composers who came to Europe such as Edward MacDowell (1861–1908), and went back speaking a foreign idiom and producing 'international' music, which at that time meant partly French, but chiefly German, followed by the generation of Copland, Thomson and others who went to Europe — in this case Paris — to try and find their musical personalities, and then returned to America to explore them to greater or lesser degrees, and then Gershwin would have been the first of the new generation of American composers for whom the pull of Europe was doubtless great, but who nevertheless found their inspiration on home soil, as composers such as Ives and Cowell had done.

However, here one is in danger of drawing Gershwin, by implication, into the 'classical' fold, and he told Cowell that as far as he was concerned, he was a man without traditions, and that as far as American music was concerned, he was history. What took

Cowell aback at first was the fact that Gershwin was incapable of hearing written music in his head. For a composer brought up in the classical tradition, it is of fundamental importance to be able to hear what the music on the page sounds like, and not just be able to read it supremely well at the keyboard, for example. Cowell paid tribute, however, to Gershwin's fantastic ear, but he had virtually no knowledge of counterpoint or harmony when Cowell first met him, and he relied almost entirely on his ear for his harmony. As Cowell admitted, most of the time he was right, but there were also occasions when he could be terribly wrong. As with Schillinger, Gershwin professed to be full of ideas, but was unable to articulate them: 'I'm crazy with ideas, and don't know what to do next.' Cowell was one of those, incidentally, who maintained that Gershwin was always in a terrible hurry, and firmly believed that he was a master of his art: 'There was tension in his music and in his voice; he was always scurrying to get the words out, always hurrying to finish one thing and get on with the next. He had tremendous gifts, but did not always know what to do with them.'

Cowell tried to persevere with Gershwin, but a composer such as Edgar Varèse (1883–1965), who had been in America from 1916 onwards, when asked by Gershwin for help, in about 1920, is said to have answered quite unequivocally: 'I can't help you. We're going in different directions. We have nothing in common musically.' That was not just Varèse distancing himself from the more popular world of Gershwin, however, since one may well imagine Varèse having said precisely the same thing to a composer such as Copland or Barber. Even if Varèse had definitely dismissed Gershwin as a musical force to be treated seriously, however, the fact remained that many composers, especially in Europe, or from the European tradition such as Schoenberg, recognized that Gershwin had given them a new dimension. Ravel was a case in point, and William Walton was another. In fact, it was through Walton that Osbert Sitwell came to know Gershwin, who would usually lunch with them when he was in London. It is from Sitwell that we have a judgement of Gershwin that may not be far short of the mark:

Many of his contemporaries, it may be, attributed an exaggerated value to his celebrated *Rhapsody in Blue*, but at least the hundreds of songs and dances [*sic*] he wrote were altogether typical in their audacity of the age that gave them birth; the

179

'twenties lived and expired to his ingenious tunes, so expert of their kind, and no chronicle of the epoch could fail to mention them and their pervasive influence.

To a large extent Osbert Sitwell was right, certainly as far as Gershwin and the Twenties were concerned, but there was *Porgy and Bess* for the Thirties, and who knows what else for the Forties and the Fifties, and so on, had Gershwin lived. It would have been sad if he had become part of the Hollywood establishment, and equally sad if he had simply lived on, writing little or nothing. Perhaps his was one of those talents that are best left with a question-mark hanging over them, and we must simply accept what is there.

Presumably, had he had a normal lifespan, there would have been more music still to come, and possibly even greater music, but that is not a very fruitful line of thought to pursue. True, there is much in *Porgy and Bess* to imply that he could have written another lyric work, given the right kind of libretto, but presumably the same might be said for Beethoven.

At the other end of the scale, having *Rhapsody in Blue* played simultaneously on eighty-four grand pianos for the opening of the 1984 Olympic Games in Los Angeles is equally consistent with the Gershwin phenomenon. He doubtless would have approved, and felt that it was an accolade he well merited. For he was, after all, a symbol, and what is more remarkable, a symbol of different things to different people, so that in the musical realm, he was able to speak to composers as different as Schoenberg and Ravel, to name but two.

To detect specific influence on other composers, however, would be rather more difficult, and although many may have emulated him, one can scarcely point to any disciples or followers. Moreover, popular music has altered so rapidly in the second half of the twentieth century that one is scarcely able to keep up with it. At present the interest in light classical music is confined to lovers of nostalgia, and those who would claim to like 'a good tune'. Gershwin certainly wrote some of those.

So finally it comes to a point of focus, a symbol, and if any one composer ever represented America in those terms, then it was George Gershwin.

Catalogue of
Works

1913

'Since I Found You' — lyrics Leonard Praskins

'Ragging the Träumerei' — lyrics Leonard Praskins

1916

'When You Want 'Em, You Can't Get 'Em, When You've Got 'Em, You Don't Want 'Em' — lyrics Murray Roth

'When the Armies Disband' — lyrics Irving Caesar [? 1918]

The Passing Show of 1916 — music mainly by Sigmund Romberg and Otto Motzan
'Making of a Girl' — Gershwin and Romberg — lyrics Harold Atteridge
Not included:
'My Runaway Girl' — lyrics Murray Roth

1917

'Rialto Ripples' — Gershwin and Will Donaldson

'Beautiful Bird' — lyrics Ira Gershwin and Lou Paley

1918

Hitchy-Koo of 1918 — music mainly by Raymond Hubbell
'You-oo Just You' — lyrics Irving Caesar

Ladies First — music mainly by A. Baldwin Sloane
'Some Wonderful Sort of Someone' — lyrics Schuyler Greene
'The Real American Folk Song' — lyrics Arthur Francis, alias Ira Gershwin

Half Past Eight
'Cupid'
'Hong Kong' — lyrics Edward B Perkins
'The Ten Commandments of Love'
'There's Magic in the Air' — lyrics Arthur Francis

'Good, Little Tune' — lyrics Irving Caesar

1919

Good Morning, Judge — music mainly by Lionel Monckton and Howard Talbot
'I Was So Young, You Were So Beautiful' — lyrics Irving Caesar and Al Bryan
'There's More to the Kiss than the X-X-X' — lyrics Irving Caesar

'O Land of Mine, America' — lyrics Michael E. Rourke

The Lady in Red — music mainly by Robert Winterberg
'Something about Love' — lyrics Lou Paley
'Some Wonderful Sort of Someone' — lyrics Schuyler Greene

La, La, Lucille — lyrics by Arthur J. Jackson and B. G. De Sylva
'From Now On'
'Nobody But You'
'Somehow it Seldom Comes True'
'Tee-Oodle-Um-Bum-Bo'
'The Best of Everything'
'There's More to the Kiss than the X-X-X' — lyrics Irving Caesar
'It's Great to Be in Love'
'It's Hard to Tell'
'The Ten Commandments of Love'
'When You Live in a Furnished Flat'
Not included:
'Kisses'
'Money, Money, Money!'
'Our Little Kitchenette'
'The Love of a Wife'

Capitol Revue ('Demi-Tasse')
'Come to the Moon' — lyrics by Lou Paley and Ned Wayburn
'Swanee' — lyrics Irving Caesar

Morris Gest Midnight Whirl — lyrics by B. G. De Sylva and John Henry Mears
'Limehouse Nights'

181

'I'll show you a Wonderful World'
'Poppyland'
'Baby Dolls'
'Doughnuts'
'Let Cutie Cut Your Cuticle'
'The League of Nations'

Lullaby — string quartet

Little Theater of our own [c. 1919]

1920

Dere Mable
  'We're Pals' — lyrics Irving Caesar
  'Yan-Kee' — lyrics Irving Caesar
  'Swanee'

Ed Wynn's Carnival — lyrics and songs
  mainly by Ed Wynn
'Oo, How I Love to Be Loved by You'
  — lyrics Lou Paley

George White's Scandals of 1920 — lyrics
  by Arthur Jackson
'Idle Dreams'
'My Lady'
'On My Mind the Whole Night Long'
'Scandal Walk'
'The Songs of Long Ago'
'Tum On and Tiss Me'
'Everybody Swat the Profiteer'
Not included:
'My Old Love Is My New Love'

The Sweetheart Shop — music mainly by
  Hugo Felix
'Waiting for the Sun to Come Out' —
  lyrics Arthur Francis

Broadway Brevities of 1920 — lyrics by
  Arthur Jackson
'Lu Lu'
'Snow Flakes'
'Spanish Love' — lyrics Irving Caesar

1921

'Dixie Rose' — lyrics Irving Caesar and
  B. G. De Sylva

'Swanee Rose' — same music as 'Dixie
  Rose', with 'Swanee' in title and lyrics

'Tomale' — lyrics B. G. De Sylva

A Dangerous Maid — lyrics by Arthur
  Francis
'Boy Wanted'
'Dancing Shoes'
'Just to Know You Are Mine'
'Some Rain Must Fall'
'The Simple Life'
Not included:
  'Anything for You'
  'The Sirens'
  'Pidgee Woo'
  'Every Girl Has a Way'

George White's Scandals of 1921 — lyrics by
  Arthur Jackson
'Drifting Along with the Tide'
'I Love You'
'She's Just a Baby'
'South Sea Isles'
'Where East Meets West'
'Mother Eve'

The Perfect Fool — book, lyrics and songs
  mainly by Ed Wynn.
'My Log-Cabin Home' — lyrics Irving
  Caesar and B. G. De Sylva
'No One Else but That Girl of Mine' —
  lyrics Irving Caesar
Figured Chorale for clarinet, two bas-
  soons, two horns, cello and bass

1922

The French Doll — book and lyrics by
  A. E. Thomas
'Do It Again' — lyrics B. G. De Sylva

For Goodness Sake — lyrics mainly by
  Arthur Jackson, music mainly by
  William Daly and Paul Lannin
'Someone' — lyrics Arthur Francis
'Tra-La-La' — lyrics Arthur Francis

Spice of 1922 — book and lyrics by Jack
  Lait
'Yankee Doodle Blues' — lyrics Irving
  Caesar and B. G. De Sylva
'The Flapper' — lyrics B. G. De Sylva

George White's Scandals of 1922 — lyrics by
  B. G. De Sylva and E. Ray Goetz
'Across the Sea'
'Argentina' — lyrics B. G. De Sylva
'Cinderelatives' — lyrics B. G. De
  Sylva
'I Found a Four Leaf Clover' — lyrics
  B. G. De Sylva
'I'll Build a Stairway to Paradise' —
  lyrics B. G. De Sylva and Arthur
  Francis
'Oh, What She Hangs Out' — lyrics
  B. G. De Sylva
'Where Is the Man of My Dreams?'
'I Can't Tell Where They're From
  When They Dance'
'Just a Tiny Cup of Tea'

Blue Monday Blues — one-act opera to
  libretto by B. G. De Sylva (orchestrated
  Will H. Vodery), later renamed *135th
  Street* (orchestrated Ferde Grofé), 1925.

Our Nell — lyrics Brian Hooker, music by
  George Gershwin and William Daly
'By and By' — music George Gershwin
'Innocent Ingenue Baby'
'My Old New England Home' — music
  George Gershwin
'Walking Home with Angeline' —

music George Gershwin
'Gol-Durn!'
'Little Villages'
'Madrigal'
'Names I Love to Hear'
'Oh, You Lady!'
'The Cooney County Fair' — music George Gershwin
'We Go to Church on Sunday' — music George Gershwin
Not included:
'The Custody of the Child'

1923

The Dancing Girl — book and lyrics by Harold Atteridge and Irving Caesar, music mainly by Sigmund Romberg
'That American Boy of Mine' — lyrics Irving Caesar

The Rainbow — lyrics mainly by Clifford Grey
'Beneath the Eastern Moon'
'Good-Night, My Dear'
'In the Rain'
'Innocent, Lonesome Blue Baby' — lyrics Brian Hooker and Clifford Grey, music George Gershwin and William Daly
'Moonlight in Versailles'
'Oh! Nina'
'Strut Lady with Me'
'Sunday in London Town'
'Sweetheart (I'm So Glad That I Met You)'
'Any Little Tune'
'Midnight Blues'

George White's Scandals of 1923 — lyrics by B. G. De Sylva, E. Ray Goetz and Ballard MacDonald
'Let's Be Lonesome Together' — lyrics B. G. De Sylva and E. Ray Goetz
'Lo-La-Lo' — lyrics B. G. De Sylva
'(On the Beach at) How've-You-Been' — lyrics B. G. De Sylva
'The Life of a Rose' — lyrics B. G. De Sylva
'There Is Nothing Too Good for You' — lyrics B. G. De Sylva and E. Ray Goetz
'Throw Her in High!' — lyrics B. G. De Sylva and E. Ray Goetz
'Where Is She?' — lyrics B. G. De Sylva
'You and I'
'Katinka'
'Laugh Your Cares Away'
'Little Scandal Dolls'
'Look in the Looking Glass'

Little Miss Bluebeard — book and lyrics by Avery Hopwood, music by George Gershwin and others

'I Won't Say I Will, But I Won't Say I Won't' — lyrics B. G. De Sylva and Arthur Francis

Nifties of 1923 — book and lyrics by William Collier and Sam Bernard, music by George Gershwin and others
'At Half Past Seven' — lyrics B. G. De Sylva
'Nashville Nightingale' — lyrics Irving Caesar

The Sunshine Trail — silent film
'The Sunshine Trail' — lyrics Arthur Francis

1924

Sweet Little Devil — lyrics by B. G. De Sylva
'Hey! Hey! Let 'Er Go!'
'Someone Who Believes in You'
'The Jijibo'
'Under a One-Man Top'
'Virginia (Don't Go Too Far)'
'Hooray for the U.S.A.'
'Just Supposing'
'Strike, Strike, Strike'
'The Matrimonial Handicap'
'The Same Old Story'
'Quite a Party'
Not included:
'Be the Life of the Crowd'
'Mah-Jongg'
'Pepita'
'Sweet Little Devil'
(You're Mighty Lucky), My Little Ducky

Rhapsody in Blue for jazz band and piano, orchestrated by Ferde Grofé

George White's Scandals of 1924 — lyrics by B. G. De Sylva
'I Need a Garden'
'I'm Going Back'
'I Love You, My Darling'
'Just Missed the Opening Chorus'
'Kongo Kate'
'Lovers of Art'
'Mah-Jongg'
'Night Time in Araby'
'Rose of Madrid'
'Somebody Loves Me' — lyrics B. G. De Sylva and Ballard MacDonald
'Tune In (to Station J.O.Y.)'
'Year after Year'

Primrose — lyrics by Desmond Carter and Ira Gershwin
'Boy Wanted'
'Isn't It Wonderful'
'Naughty Baby'
'Some Far-Away Someone' — lyrics Ira Gershwin and B. G. De Sylva (the

tune is the same as 'At Half Past Seven' from *Nifties of 1923*)
'That New-Fangled Mother of Mine' — lyrics Desmond Carter
'This is the Life for a Man' — lyrics Desmond Carter
'Wait a Bit, Susie' — ballet
'Beau Brummel' — lyrics Desmond Carter
'I'll Have a House in Berkeley Square, I'll Have a Cottage at Kew' — lyrics Desmond Carter
'Can We Do Anything?'
'Four Little Sirens' — lyrics Ira Gershwin, revised version of 'The Sirens', not included in *A Dangerous Maid* (1921)
'I Make Hay When the Moon Shines' — lyrics Desmond Carter
'Isn't It Terrible What They Did to Mary Queen of Scots' — lyrics Desmond Carter
'It Is the Fourteenth of July' — lyrics Desmond Carter
'Roses of France' — lyrics Desmond Carter
'The Mophams' — lyrics Desmond Carter
'Till I Meet Someone Like You' — lyrics Desmond Carter
'When Toby Is Out of Town' — lyrics Desmond Carter

Lady, Be Good — lyrics Ira Gershwin
'Fascinating Rhythm'
'Hang on to me'
'Carnival Time'
'Leave it to Love'
'Little Jazz Bird'
'Oh, Lady, Be Good!'
'So Am I'
'The Half of It, Dearie, Blues'
'A Wonderful Party'
'Juanita'
'Seeing Dickie Home'
'Swiss Miss' — lyrics Ira Gershwin and Arthur Jackson
'The End of a String'
'The Robinson Hotel'
'We're Here Because'
Not included:
'The Man I Love'
'Evening Star'
'Rainy Afternoon Girls'
'Singin' Pete'
'The Bad, Bad Men'
'Weather Man'
'Will You Remember Me?'
Added for 1926 London production — 'I'd Rather Charleston' — lyrics Desmond Carter
'Something about Love' — lyrics Lou Paley

'Buy a Little Button from Us' — lyrics Desmond Carter

1925
Short Story — arrangement, by Samuel Dushkin, of two 'Novelettes' for piano, for violin and piano

Tell Me More — lyrics by B. G. De Sylva and Ira Gershwin
'Baby!'
'Kickin' the Clouds Away'
'My Fair Lady'
'Why Do I Love You?'
'Tell Me More!'
'Three Times a Day'
'How Can I Win You Now?'
'In Sardinia'
'Love Is in the Air'
'Mr and Mrs Sipkin'
'The Poetry of Motion'
'Ukulele Lorelei'
'When the Debbies Go By'
Not included — 'I'm Somethin' on Avenue A'
'Once'
'Shop Girls and Mannikins'
'The He-Man'
Added for 1925 London production — 'Murderous Monty (and Light-Fingered Jane)' — lyrics Desmond Carter
'Love, I Never Knew'

Concerto in F for piano and orchestra

Tip-Toes — lyrics by Ira Gershwin
'Looking for a Boy'
'Nice Baby! (Come to Papa!)'
'Nightie-Night'
'Sweet and Low-Down'
'That Certain Feeling'
'These Charming People'
'When Do We Dance?'
'Harbor of Dreams'
'Lady Luck'
'Our Little Captain'
'Tip-Toes'
'Waiting for the Train'
Not included:
'It's a Great Little World!'
'Dancing Hour'
'Gather Ye Rosebuds'
'Harlem River Chanty'
'Life's Too Short to Be Blue'
'We'

Song of the Flame — book and lyrics by Oscar Hammerstein II and Otto Harbach, music by George Gershwin and Herbert Stothart
'Cossack Love Song (Don't Forget Me)'
'Midnight Bells' — music George Gershwin

184

'Song of the Flame'
'The Signal' — music George Gershwin
'Vodka, Don't Give Me Vodka'
'Far Away'
'Tar-Tar'
'Women's Work is Never Done'
Not included:
'You Are You'

1926

Americana — book and lyrics by J. P.
McEvoy, music by George Gershwin and others
'That Lost Barber Shop Chord' —
lyrics Ira Gershwin

Oh, Kay! — lyrics by Ira Gershwin
'Clap Yo' Hands'
'Dear Little Girl' — omitted after
first performance
'Do, Do, Do'
'Fidgety Feet'
'Heaven on Earth' — lyrics Ira Ger-
shwin and Howard Dietz
'Maybe'
'Oh, Kay' — lyrics Ira Gershwin
and Howard Dietz
'Someone to Watch over Me'
'Bride and Groom'
'Don't Ask!'
'The Woman's Touch'
Not included:
'Show Me the Town'
'Ain't It Romantic?'
'Bring on the Ding Dong Dell'
'Guess Who' — music same as for
'Don't Ask!'
'Stepping with Baby'
'The Moon Is on the Sea'
'The Sun is on the Sea'
'What's the Use?'
'When Our Ship Comes Sailing In'

Preludes for Piano — five composed
this year, three of which were published in 1927 as *Preludes for Piano*.

1927

Strike Up the Band (first version) —
lyrics by Ira Gershwin
'Military Dancing Drill'
'Seventeen and Twenty-One'
'Strike Up the Band!'
'The Man I Love'
'Yankee Doodle Rhythm'
'Fletcher's American Cheese Choral
Society'
'Homeward Bound'

'Hoping That Someday You'll Care'
'How About a Man Like Me'
'Meadow Serenade'
'Oh, This Is Such a Lovely War'
'Patriotic Rally'
'The Girl I Love'
'The Unofficial Spokesman'
'The War That Ended War'
'Typical Self-Made American'

Funny Face — lyrics by Ira Gershwin
'Dance Alone with You'
'Funny Face'
'He Loves and She Loves'
'High Hat'
'Let's Kiss and Make Up'
'My One and Only (What Am I
Gonna Do)'
' 'S Wonderful'
'The Babbit and the Bromide'
'Blue Hullaballoo'
'The World Is Mine'
'Birthday Party'
'Come Along, Let's Gamble'
'If You Will Take Our Tip'
'Tell the Doc'
'The Finest of the Finest'
'Those Eyes'
Not included:
'We're All A-Worry, All Agog'
'When You're Single'
'How Long Has This Been Going
On?'
'Acrobats'
'In the Swim'
'Once'
'Sing a Little Song'
'Dancing Hour'
'The World is Mine'
'Come Along, Let's Gamble'

1928

Rosalie — lyrics by Ira Gershwin and
P. G. Wodehouse, additional
music by Sigmund Romberg
'Ev'rybody Knows I Love Some-
body' — lyrics Ira Gershwin, tune
same as 'Dance Alone with You'
from *Funny Face*
'How Long Has This Been Going
On?' — lyrics Ira Gershwin
'Oh Gee! Oh Joy!'
'Say So!'
'Let Me Be a Friend to You' — lyrics
Ira Gershwin
'New York Serenade' — lyrics Ira
Gershwin

'Show Me the Town' — lyrics by Ira
Gershwin
Not included:
'Beautiful Gypsy' — lyrics Ira Ger-
shwin, tune same as 'Wait a Bit,
Susie' from *Primrose*
'Rosalie' — lyrics Ira Gershwin
'Yankee Doodle Rhythm' — lyrics
Ira Gershwin
'Follow the Drum' — lyrics Ira Ger-
shwin
'I Forgot What I Started to Say' —
lyrics Ira Gershwin
'The Man I Love' — lyrics Ira Ger-
shwin
'You Know How It Is'
'When Cadets Parade' — lyrics Ira
Gershwin

Treasure Girl — lyrics Ira Gershwin
'Feeling I'm Falling'
'Got a Rainbow'
'I Don't Think I'll Fall in Love To-
day'
'I've Got a Crush on You'
'K-ra-zy for You'
'Oh, So Nice'
'What Are We Here For?'
'Where's the Boy? Here's the Girl!'
'According to Mr Grimes'
'Place in the Country'
'Skull and Bones'
Not included:
'A Hunting We Will Go'
'Dead Men Tell No Tales'
'Good-Bye to the Old Love, Hello to
the New'
'I Want to Marry a Marionette'
'This Particular Party'
'Treasure Island'
'What Causes That?'

An American in Paris, tone poem for
orchestra

1929

Show Girl — lyrics by Ira Gershwin and
Gus Kahn
'Do What You Do!'
'Harlem Serenade'
'I Must Be Home by Twelve
O'Clock'
'Liza (All the Cloud'll Roll Away)'
'So Are You'
'An American in Paris' — ballet
'Black and White'
'Follow the Minstrel Band'

'Happy Birthday'
'Home Blues'
'How Could I Forget'
'Lolita, My Love'
'My Sunday Fella'
'One Man'
Not included:
'Feeling Sentimental'
'Adored One'
'At Mrs Simpkin's Finishing School'
'Home Lovin' Gal'
'Home Lovin' Man'
'I Just Looked at You'
'I'm Just a Bundle of Sunshine'
'I'm Out for No Good Reason To-
night'
'Minstrel Show'
'Somebody Stole My Heart Away'
'Someone's Always Calling a Re-
hearsal'
'Tonight's the Night'

East is West:
Proposed Ziegfeld musical (to be called
Ming Toy) which was never pro-
duced. Gershwin wrote the following
songs — lyrics by Ira Gershwin:
'In the Mandarin's Orchid Garden'
'We are Visitors'
'Embraceable You'
'Sing Song Girl'
'Impromptu in Two Keys' — in-
strumental, no lyrics
'China Girl'
'Lady of the Moon'

1930

Strike Up the Band (second version) —
lyrics by Ira Gershwin
'Hangin' Around with You'
'I Mean to Say'
'I Want to Be a War Bride'
'I've Got a Crush on You'
'Mademoiselle in New Rochelle'
'Soon'
'Strike Up the Band'
'A Man of High Degree'
'A Typical Self-Made American'
'Fletcher's American Chocolate
Choral Society Workers'
'First There Was Fletcher'
'He Knows Milk'
'How About A Boy Like Me?'
'If I Became the President'
'In the Rattle of the Battle'
'Military Dancing Drill'

'Ring a Ding a Ding Dong Bell'
'The Unofficial Spokesman'
'This Could Go On for Years'
'Three Cheers for the Union!'
'Unofficial March of General Holmes'
Not included:
'There Was Never Such a Charming War'

Girl Crazy — lyrics by Ira Gershwin
'Bidin' My Time'
'Boy! What Love Has Done to Me!'
'But Not for Me'
'Could You Use Me?'
'Embraceable You'
'I Got Rhythm'
'Sam and Delilah'
'Treat Me Rough'
'Barbary Coast'
'Broncho Busters'
'Goldfarb! That's I'm!'
'Land of the Gay Caballero'
'The Lonesome Cowboy'
'When It's Cactus Time in Arizona'
Not included:
'And I Have You'
'Something Peculiar'
'The Gambler of the West'
'You Can't Unscramble Scrambled Eggs'

1931

Delicious (film) — lyrics by Ira Gershwin
'Blah-Blah-Blah'
'Delishious'
'Katinkitschka'
'Somebody from Somewhere'
A dream sequence — 'We're from the *Journal* . . . '
A rhapsody (excerpt from what became the *Second Rhapsody*)
Not included:
'Mischa, Yascha, Toscha, Sascha'

Of Thee I Sing — lyrics by Ira Gershwin
'Because, Because'
'How Beautiful'
'Love is Sweeping the Country'
'Of Thee I Sing'
'The Illegitimate Daughter'
'Who Cares?'
'Wintergreen for President'
'Here's a Kiss for Cinderella'
'Garçon, S'il Vous Plaît'

'Entrance of the French Ambassador'
'Hello, Good Morning'
'I Was the Most Beautiful Blossom'
'I'm About to Be a Mother (Who Could Ask for Anything More?)'
'Jilted, Jilted!'
'Never Was There a Girl So Fair'
'On That Matter No One Budges'
'Posterity is Just Around the Corner'
'Some Girls Can Bake a Pie'
'The Dimple on My Knee'
'The Senatorial Roll Call'
'Trumpeter, Blow Your Horn'
'Who is the Lucky Girl to Be?'
Not included:
'Call Me Whate'er You Will'

1932

Second Rhapsody, for orchestra with piano

'You've Got What Gets Me' — lyrics by Ira Gershwin, for film version of *Girl Crazy*

Cuban Overture (*Rumba*), for orchestra

George Gershwin's Song Book, piano transcriptions of following songs:
'Swanee'
'Nobody But You'
'I'll Build a Stairway to Paradise'
'Do It Again'
'Fascinating Rhythm'
'Oh, Lady, Be Good!'
'Somebody Loves Me'
'Sweet and Low-Down'
'That Certain Feeling'
'The Man I Love'
'Clap Yo' Hands'
'Do, Do, Do'
'My One and Only'
' 'S Wonderful'
'Strike Up the Band'
'Liza'
'I Got Rhythm'
'Who Cares?'

1933

Pardon My English — lyrics by Ira Gershwin
'Isn't It a Pity'
'I've Got to Be There'
'Lorelei'
'Luckiest Man in the World'
'My Cousin in Milwaukee'
'So What?'

187

'Where You Go, I Go'
'Dancing in the Streets'
'Hail the Happy Couple'
'He's Not Himself'
'In Three-Quarter Time'
'Pardon My English'
'The Dresden Northwest Mounted'
'Tonight'
'What Sort of Wedding Is This?'
Not included:
  'Bauer's House'
  'Fatherland, Mother of the Band'
  'Freud and Jung and Adler'
  'Poor Michael! Poor Golo!'
  'Together at Last'

Let 'Em Eat Cake — lyrics by Ira Gershwin
'Blue, Blue, Blue'
'Let 'Em Eat Cake'
'Mine'
'On and On and On'
'Union Square'
'A Hell of a Hole'
'Climb Up the Social Ladder'
'Cloistered from the Noisy City'
'Comes the Revolution'
'Double Dummy Drill'
'Down with Everything That's Up'
'Hanging Throttlebottom in the Morning'
'I Knew a Foul Ball'
'Let 'Em Eat Caviar'
'Oyez, Oyez, Oyez'
'No Comprenez, No Capish, No Versteh!'
'Shirts by the Millions'
'That's What He Did'
'The Union League'
'Throttle Throttlebottom'
'Tweedledee for President'
'Up and at 'Em! On to Vict'ry'
'What More Can a General Do?'
'Why Speak of Money?'
'Wintergreen for President'
'Who's the Greatest . . .?'
Not included:
  'First Lady and First Gent'
  'Till Then'

1934

'I Got Rhythm' Variations, for piano and orchestra

1935

Porgy and Bess, libretto by DuBose Heyward, lyrics by DuBose Heyward

and Ira Gershwin
Overture — Act I
'Summertime'
'A Woman Is a Sometime Thing'
'Here Comes de Honey Man'
'They Pass By Singin' '
'Crap Game Fugue'
'Oh Little Stars'
'Crown and Robbins' Fight'
'Gone, Gone, Gone'
'Overflow'
'My Man's Gone Now'
'Leavin' fo' the Promis' Lan' '

Act II
'It Takes a Long Pull to Get There'
'I Got Plenty o' Nuttin' '
'Woman to Lady'
'Bess, You Is My Woman Now'
'Oh, I Can't Sit Down'
'It Ain't Necessarily So'
'What You Want wid Bess?'
'Time and Time Again'
'Street Cries (Strawberry Woman, Crab Man)'
'I Loves You, Porgy'
'Storm Music'
'Oh, de Lawd Shake de Heaven'
'A Red-Headed Woman'
'Oh, Doctor Jesus'

Act III
'Clara, (Don't You Be Downhearted)'
'There's a Boat Dat's Leavin' Soon for New York'
'Oh, Bess, Oh Where's My Bess?'
'I'm On My Way' (later dropped)

Not included:
  'Jasbo Brown Blues' (piano music)
  'Buzzard Song'
  'I Hates Yo' Struttin' Style'
  'I Ain't Got No Shame'
  'Oh, Hev'nly Father'
  'Good Mornin', Sistuh! Good Mornin', Brudder!'
  'Sure to Go To Heaven'

1936

Catfish Row, suite in five movements adapted from *Porgy and Bess*:
'Catfish Row'
'Porgy Sings'
'Fugue'
'Hurricane'
'Good Morning, Brother'

'King of Swing' — lyrics Albert Stillman

'Strike Up the Band for U.C.L.A.' — lyrics Ira Gershwin

The Show Is On — lyrics by Ira Gershwin and others, music by George Gershwin and others
'By Strauss' — lyrics Ira Gershwin

1937

Shall We Dance (film) — lyrics by Ira Gershwin
'(I've Got) Beginner's Luck'
'Let's Call the Whole Thing Off'
'Shall We Dance'
'Slap That Bass'
'They All Laughed'
'They Can't Take That Away from Me'
Instrumental interlude — 'Walking the Dog'
Not included:
'Hi-Ho'
'Wake Up, Brother, and Dance'

A Damsel in Distress (film) — lyrics by Ira Gershwin
'A Foggy Day'
'I Can't Be Bothered Now'
'Nice Work If You Can Get It'
'Stiff Upper Lip'
'The Jolly Tar and the Milk Maid'
'Things are Looking Up'
'Put Me to the Test'
'Sing of Spring'
Not included:
'Pay Some Attention to Me'

1938

The Goldwyn Follies (film) — lyrics by Ira Gershwin
'I Love to Rhyme'
'I Was Doing All Right'

'Love Is Here to Stay'
'Love Walked In'
Not included:
'Just Another Rumba'

'Dawn of a New Day' — lyrics Ira Gershwin (posthumous, completed with Kay Swift's help)

1946

The Shocking Miss Pilgrim (film) — lyrics by Ira Gershwin, music by George Gershwin (posthumous, adapted by Kay Swift with Ira Gershwin)
'Aren't You Kind of Glad We Did?'
'Changing My Tune'
'For You, For Me, For Evermore'
'One, Two, Three'
'The Back Bay Polka'
'Demon Rum'
'Stand Up and Fight'
'Sweet Packard'
'Waltzing Is Better Sitting Down'
'Welcome Song'
Not included:
'Tour of the Town'

1964

Kiss Me, Stupid (film) — lyrics by Ira Gershwin, music by George Gershwin (posthumous, adapted by Ira Gershwin)
'All the Livelong Day'
'I'm a Poached Egg'
'Sophia' (based on 'Wake Up, Brother, and Dance', not included in *Shall We Dance* (1937)

1971

Two Waltzes in C, for piano (based on a sequence written for *Pardon My English* [1933], but not included)

For a very full bibliography, the reader is directed to Charles Schwartz's *Gershwin: His Life and Music*, New York and Indianapolis, 1973 — paperback edition 1979. Only a few of the more accessible books are listed here.

ARMITAGE, M., ed., *George Gershwin*, New York, 1938

EWEN, D., *George Gershwin. A Journey to Greatness*, New York and London, 1956. Revised ed. 1970 as *George Gershwin: His Journey to Greatness*, Englewood Cliffs, New Jersey

GERSHWIN, I., *Lyrics on Several Occasions*, New York, 1959, 2nd ed. 1973, London, 1977

GOLDBERG, E., *George Gershwin: A Study in American Music*, New York, 1931; revised ed. 1958

JABLONSKI, E., and Stewart, L.D., *The Gershwin Years*, New York, 1958; revised ed. 1973

KIMBALL, R., and Simon, A., *The Gershwins*, New York, 1973

PAYNE, R., *Gershwin*, New York, 1960; London 1962

Selective Index

(see also Catalogue of Works)

190

His Majesty's Theatre

Proprietor .... JOSEPH BENSON
Licensed by the Lord Chamberlain to WILLIAM CLIFFORD GAUNT

EVERY EVENING AT 8.15
MATINEES : THURSDAY AND SATURDAY AT 2.30

MUSICAL PLAYS
In conjunction with ALEX. A. AARONS and VINTON FR

present

GERTRUDE LAWRENCE
in

"OH, KAY!"
A New Musical Comedy

BOOK by GUY BOLTON and P. G. WODEHOUSE
LYRICS by IRA GERSHWIN
MUSIC by GEORGE GERSHWIN

Characters (in the order of their appearance):

Molly .... RITA Mc
Peggy .... REITA N
Dolly Ruxton .... BETH D
Phillippa Ruxton .... BETTY
The Duke of Datchet ...... CLAUD
Chauffeur .... JACK D
Jimmy Winter .... HAROL
Constance Appleton
"Shorty" McGee
Larry Potter
Kay
Revenue Officer Jansen
Judge Appleton

Ladies:
VERA BUDGE
ERIN BURKE
PAT CHARLES
VIVIAN CALMAINE
KATHLEEN DAW
JEWELEEN DAW
DOROTHY DOBSON
RUBY DUFFIS
OLIVE FIRTH
ROSAMUND GARDNER

CONNIE HARRIS
MOLLY HARTLEY
LENA HOLMES
KATHLEEN JOYCE
VERA LINGLEY
ELISE LINGLEY
PAMBASTON
VI MARSDEN
MADGE MARTIN
RENA MAY
MABS NEWNHAM
BETTY NEWNHAM

Gentlemen:
L. CAMERON
DOUGLAS CHALLONER
FRANK FOX
E. GIFFORD

W. H. KEARTON
THOMAS LOWE
FRED LE ROY
L. NAISMITH
ALFRED OSBOR

EMPIRE THEATRE
LEICESTER SQUARE :: :: LONDON, W.C.2
Managing Director .... ALFRED BUTT
Manager .... OSCAR BARRETT

The Management politely request that, where necessary,
LADIES WILL REMOVE THEIR HATS,
in order not to obstruct the view of those sitting behind

TWICE DAILY at 2.30 and 8.30

"THE RAINBOW
The New Empire Revue

By ALBERT de COURVILLE, EDGAR WALLACE and NOEL
Lyrics by CLIFFORD GREY Music by GEORGE GERS
Dances and Ensembles by ALLAN K. FOSTER

Produced by ALBERT de COURVILLE

DAPHNE POLLARD

GRACE HAYES   ERNEST THES

STEPHANIE STEPHENS

Empire Theatre

FRED and ADELE

ALFRED BUTT
with
ALEX. A. AARONS and VINTON FREEDLEY
presents

FRED and ADELE ASTAIRE
in

A New Musical Comedy

"LADY, BE GOOD!"

Book by GUY BOLTON and FRED THOMPSON
Music by GEORGE GERSHWIN
Lyrics by IRA GERSHWIN
Dances and Ensembles staged by MAX SCHECK

The Characters in order of their appearance:

Bertie Bassett .... EWART SCOTT
Daisy Parke .... GLORI BEAUMONT
Dick Trevor .... FRED ASTAIRE
Susie Trevor .... ADELE ASTAIRE
.... STOWELL

His Majesty's
Theatre

GERTRUDE LAWRENCE
in
"OH, KAY!"

THE MAGAZINE—PROGRAMME

Winter Garden Theatre
DRURY LANE, W.C.2
Licensed by the Lord Chamberlain to
GEORGE GROSSMITH and J. A. E. MALONE

Every Evening at 8 15   Matinees : Thursday and Saturday at 2.15

GEORGE GROSSMITH & J. A. E. MALONE
present
HEATHER THATCHER
PERCY HEMING   MARGERY HICKLIN
and
LESLIE HENSON
in a New MUSICAL COMEDY in Three Acts

PRIMROSE

BOOK by GEORGE GROSSMITH and GUY BOLTON
LYRICS by DESMOND CARTER
MUSIC by GEORGE GERSHWIN
(By arrangement with ALEX A. AARONS and VINTON FREEDLEY)

Characters in the Order in which they Appear:

Jason .... Mr. ERNEST GRAHAM
Freddie Falls .... Mr. CLAUDE HULBERT
May Rooker .... Miss VERA LENNOX
Sir Benjamin Falls ...... Mr. GUY FANE
Joan (his Ward) .... Miss MARGERY HICKLIN
Hilliary Vane (a Novelist) Mr. PERCY HEMING
Toby Mopham .... Mr. LESLIE HENSON
Michael .... Mr. THOMAS WEGUELIN
Manager of Hotel .... Mr. HAROLD BRADLEY
Tie Peach (Mdme. Frazeline) Miss HEATHER THATCHER
Sophia Mopham .... Miss SYLVIA HAWKES

Villagers, River Girls, Sports Girls, Sportsmen, Visitors, &c.:

MIGNON MORENZA   Hon. Dally   MARGARET MOORE
ESME de VAYNE   Miss Tishy   GERALDINE AYLMER
WINIFRED SHOTTER   Miss Tony   PHYLLIS GARTON
KATHLEEN BURGIS   Marie   DOROTHY DAW
BERYL MURRAY   Cutre   SYBIL EASTLEY
LEILA MURRAY   Blush   BUBBLES RYAN
MOLLY VERE   Witch Hazel   ESTELLE DYAN
DOROTHY DEANE   1st Ballerina   ELAINE PEDLARS
YVONNE O'BEARE   and   DAISY DALZELL
PHYLLIS SWINBURNE   3rd   AUDREY CARLTON
Y, MAISIE GLYN, ISS GLADYS SUMMITT, PEGGY BLAKE, MARIE LYNNE

LESLIE FRENCH   Jorrocks   FRED. WHITLOCK
GUY SAUNDERS   De Travers   FRANK BROWN
RALPH RUTLAND   Agent de Police JACK MORGAN
GEORGE HAMILTON   The Colonel   JACK WERNDLEY
P. WILSON BARRETT   The Captain   JOHN REDMOND

Act II. appears by arrangement with " The Trocadero"

THE COMPETITIONS ON PAGES 17 & 19